EGO
FEAR AND
FILMMAKING

A SURVIVAL GUIDE
FOR CREATIVES

RON McPHERSON

Audio book available at:

CreativeHQ.com

Download the bonus materials at:

CreativeHQ.com/bonus

ISBN 978-1-09839-556-8 (Print)

ISBN 978-1-09839-557-5 (eBook)

This book is dedicated to Frankie, the love of my life.
And to you, the Dreamers that believe in magic.

TABLE OF CONTENTS

Introduction 1

CHAPTER 1 The Wild West 3

CHAPTER 2 So, You Want to Be a Director? 15

CHAPTER 3 Ego and the Addiction to Fear 34

CHAPTER 4 The Journey of Your Film 48

CHAPTER 5 Time & Money 61

CHAPTER 6 Why You're Losing Money 73

CHAPTER 7 Bringing Sexy Back 86

CHAPTER 8 Creative Health Becomes Creative Wealth 93

CHAPTER 9 Hire Yourself 101

CHAPTER 10 Live Happily Ever After 107

INTRODUCTION

I'm so glad that you're reading this; I promise it will be worth it. If you're going to be working with cameras, lighting and sound, you're going to be a storyteller. And you're in the right place.

I'm so grateful to be making a living doing what I love. I've been around the world making all kinds of movies, and I work with incredible artists. When it comes to making successful, fun and profitable content, you've got to have a great strategy. I want to help creatives be their best, by sharing what I've learned. When I was struggling, I didn't have anyone that could really help, and I wanted to change that for others. I'm going to give you some solutions and strategies that really work. I'm going to be your guide on *your* creative adventure.

This is going to save you *time, money and a lot of frustration*.

We're going to be taking a deep look at some things that may surprise you. We're going to look at how we get in those rough situations and who we are going through them. We'll discover why you're not where you think you should be right now *and how to get there faster*.

I'm going to give you some tools that are going to help you get what you really want. I'll teach you strategies that will get you on track in a *fast, healthy* way. You have to do the work and remember it's a practice. That means you practice it daily, the best you can.

We're going to talk about how Hollywood is a Grand Illusion—it's not what you think. It's magic; it's where we work. Your real success begins with an inside job. Everything that comes from you creatively starts *inside*. We're going to be tapping into exactly how that works

1

for you. This is a real superpower that you have. We all have it, and the world will always need more of it.

If you have a crappy day or an epic fail, you begin again. This is what we're going to train for and I'm so glad you're here.

But how do we start? One of the hardest parts is *starting*. And you've already done that, so congratulations!

The adventure begins.

CHAPTER 1
THE WILD WEST

Being a freelance filmmaker can be like living in the Wild West. Everyone's a gun for hire, you'll be traveling into all kinds of different towns, meeting interesting people and shooting them, with a camera. You'll brave stretches of rough terrain and harsh weather. And, you'll be doing this with equipment that usually can't get dirty or wet. When things go right, you get the credit. When things go wrong, someone else gets the blame. You'll encounter people that are "in charge" but lack serious leadership skills.

Nobody gets to tell you what to do in the Wild West. You represent everything—you are the company and the talent, and you're taking the risk. There's no real "freelancer union" or labor board that truly has your back. And the "rules" you might have heard from one or two people might end up to be more like myths, or distortions of the truth. Just like the real Wild West.

You're going to need to be prepared to deal with all kinds of people. You'll need to be ready, in case you end up in a shoot-out, or what we might call creative differences. After all, this is how you make a living, and if your pay gets held up, things can get heated very fast. Next, we're going to talk about what you might encounter and how to prepare for your own safety, health and prosperity.

Let's not forget about the fun factor as well. We make movies and tell stories because it's fun! When it stops becoming fun, you may be getting into some trouble. Here's how you're able to tell.

ASK YOURSELF WHY YOU ARE DOING A CERTAIN PROJECT OR WORKING WITH A SPECIFIC PERSON?

If your answer is "because I need the money," then that would be the first red flag. I personally have spent years chasing the money, and I can tell you it doesn't work. The bottom line is you end up prostituting your skills and talents, and it's always a temporary patch that really ends up being what I call the hamster wheel. You know the little wheel that hamsters just run in place on and don't go anywhere? Yet they're exhausting all their energy. That's what happens when you chase money. You will likely get swept into a vortex of busyness, and the last thing on your mind will be course correcting. You'll be distracted paying all the bills and meeting demands, all the while running on the hamster wheel. If you try to tell someone they're on the hamster wheel they might be easily offended because they have to keep running. There're bills to be paid, deadlines and some stressed-out drama that's likely around the corner. And we're looking forward to this. After all, it's just "how the business works." Or at least that's the story we're telling ourselves. Are you telling yourself some version of this story?

Start to question your sacrifices and where you're putting your energy.

Here're a few questions to ask yourself:

★ What are the benefits to me?

★ Whom and/or what am I sacrificing time away from to do this?

★ Am I enjoying the people and the process?

★ Am I using my superpowers or being a victim?

WE SHOULD BE ASKING, WHY DO WE ALLOW OURSELVES TO BE OUR CAREER'S BITCH?

It's easy to blame money and always be busy, multitask and totally sell out to our career. We even claim it: "I'm a workaholic." So you're married to your job? "Yep, that's my life." I can't tell you how many times I've heard some version of this. And yet, a lot of those same people aren't really happy with what they're making, whom they're working with and how the journey is happening. How do I know this? Because I was one of those people.

It's the hamster wheel. When we're so busy and wrapped up in everything that's coming at us, there's no time for balance or meditation. Ha! And you can forget eating healthy or sometimes even eating at all.

There's just no time for it. We just jump back on the hamster wheel. Maybe it's unspoken, so I'll say it. If I'm busy, I don't have to deal with certain things. If I'm busy, they'll understand why it's not the way it should be. If I'm busy, you need to cut me some slack. It's the reason that when people say it, they usually lead with it. "Hey, I've been so busy...." And then the conversation begins from there.

It's incredibly refreshing to know people that are never too busy for you. It just feels good knowing you have someone's full attention and it only takes a little more awareness. Anyone can do it. Imagine talking to your favorite celebrity or someone important and they were only 40% in the conversation because 60% of their energy was elsewhere. The real professionals that I've seen under pressure that take the time and give their full attention always get a more satisfying result. Imagine giving 100% of your attention to a project or a person in the time you have. People know when you give them 100% of your attention; they can feel it. This earns respect and builds trust. You will positively stand out and be remembered. This is an essential for directors and leaders.

Professionals like Kevin Hart make it a point to say hello to everyone on the crew and thank them. Even though he's busy— he's got lines to remember— he has an awareness. You can imagine the cool impression it leaves on people too.

GIVING YOUR FULL ATTENTION TO OTHERS IS A SUPERPOWER.

You're about to learn some powerful tools for raising your artist awareness. Many of us are gifted and very much in tune with creative frequencies. And some of you are going to find how to better communicate with your inner artist. It's kinda funny to actually catch yourself in these crazy moments or even on the hamster wheel. And that's progress. You might have spent weeks or months on the hamster wheel before. As you're practicing raising your artist awareness, you'll notice you're saving loads of time and energy.

In the Wild West, you'll encounter varying displays of uncontrollable attention deficit's. You'll recognize these characters easily. Most of them will just tell you, "I'm super ADD, but I'm listening." They usually say that while trying to have a conversation with you and a couple others at the same time. You might even have to give them a second because they're just handling something important. We'll be talking about doing business with some of these colorful characters and how to stay protected and less frustrated.

UNDERPROMISE AND OVERDELIVER. ONE OF THE THINGS THAT STILL HOLDS TRUE, ESPECIALLY IN THE WILD WEST, IS YOUR WORD. YOUR WORD IS YOUR BOND; IT'S ALL YOU'VE GOT. YOUR WORD IS POWERFUL AND EARNS TRUST.

In the Wild West, people wore guns. Why? Well, for a lot of reasons. You could say protection is what comes to mind first. And you'd be right because survival in the Wild West means you don't know whom you can trust. In fact, you were probably taught don't trust anyone. But eventually, somehow, you'll start trusting people. And they'll start trusting you. They'll trust you with things of great importance, even their lives.

CREATIVE HEALTH = CREATIVE WEALTH

I know a lot a wealthy people that don't have big bank accounts. They happen to be wealthy in a lot of other areas. Creatively, you can be very wealthy, and it has nothing to do with what's in your bank account. The idea that we've been programmed to believe that we have to have a certain amount of money to be wealthy is actually a myth. I know several wealthy people that are just not visual people. They're not creative in the same way, yet when we combine our resources, projects get made. Is it possible to have one without the other? Actually, there's another way to look at it. I would ask, what can I contribute? Is it possible to make a profit and have a great journey? If you ask these questions about everything you're embarking upon, you'll be using another superpower. In fact, you'll be determining your future.

Sometimes the answers (or the outlook) are uncertain.

Learn to find comfort in uncertainty; it's where creativity thrives. Rather than fear it, trust it. Some of my best experiences in filmmaking have come from not knowing exactly how I was going to make something work out. When you surround yourself with the right people, you always find a way together. It's because you share a trust, a belief in the project and each other. This is why, especially on really hard projects, when they come to an end, we're glad but also sad. We're sad that we'll be saying goodbye to our film family. Because that's the part we cherish the most. Sure we got great shots; we did all this and had all that. But the people you connect with, what you'll learn and the experiences you'll share are priceless. That's why certain teams just go from project to project together. They have their people that they trust. There's that word again—trust. What happens when a new person is hired that hasn't been on the team before? That person is instantly trusted if they were recommended by a trusted person. When I break it down, it's simple. I encourage productions to hire specific people because we won't have to worry. When they say, "But they're too expensive," I remind them to think of the extra expense like an insurance policy. You'll have far less risk and worry because you know whom you're investing in. It's the closest guarantee I can give a production that helps minimize risk. I present the facts, but production decides based on the risk and budget, and we go from there.

DON'T BE SO QUICK TO TAKE ON ALL OF A PROJECT'S BURDENS. STRATEGIZE AND DELEGATE.

I was filming a music video that was using a Steadicam for most of the day. And the Steadicam operator I got was a recommendation. They came from a trusted source. I had used this person before and everything went great, so there was no real concerns.

Fast forward to us on location about 90 minutes outside of Los Angeles. We were on a mountain top with little to no phone reception. The coastal location was expensive and delicate in how you could move around it. We had to take a lot of extra precaution to avoid potential damage. When a crew of 40 to 50 people come to your house, it's easy for wear and tear to occur. When it came to filming, my Steadicam operator had to break the shot after just a minute or so because of some back pain. So we stopped and waited a bit, I checked on him and when he was ready, we continued. We weren't flying a heavy camera setup, so I knew it wasn't too much weigh to deal with. After a couple more attempts, he mentioned he had pulled his back from another shoot he did earlier in the week and it was just catching up with him. This is a tricky situation where there was no insurance that production had that covered this sort of loss or delay. Even when they do, it's really expensive and most independents can't afford this addition to the policy. And I want to remind you that a lot of music videos are self-funded by the artists. It's the artist's hard-earned money that we are trusted with. This was a pretty unusual circumstance, and the clock was ticking. There it was again, UNCERTAINTY, right in my face.

So now what? I was very understanding and kind, and I went to the director, who mirrored that sympathy. And while it was frustrating and I wasn't able to get the shots the way I had planned, the saving grace was how we came through it. It would have been real easy to start blaming or saying, he should not have charged you or given a big discount on his rate for that day. But instead we recognized the hand we'd been dealt and did the best we could, safely. We took the time, worked together and got through it. A couple weeks later, we came back with just a few people to shoot pick-up shots. I was able to give a great discount to help the client and the filming location did as well. When we finished, we all felt like we had even more incredible shots than the first day, even though we had 80% less time, money and crew. It's because we trusted uncertainty rather than fearing it, and we moved through it with grace.

The practices that you're learning right now support your creative health. You're raising your artist awareness and growing your superpowers. When you do things that support your creative health, it pays off in creative wealth. The nose-to-the-grindstone attitude and surviving on junk food with little sleep is not supporting creative health and is often creating a longer and more frustrating journey.

When you're looking for work or are in the process of accepting work, it's good to have a checklist FOR YOU. I consider it a Hero Checklist. We'll talk about productions agreements later; that is different.

Here's my personal checklist when I'm hired as a director of photography on a film. Take a look at how trust plays a large role in my process. Often times, the job is a referral, like most of my new projects, and I don't really know the potential client.

If you do these six things, it's like having a crystal ball and looking into the future of your journey.

THE HERO CHECKLIST:

1. Do I like the script and the concept?

2. What value can I bring to the project?

3. Do I get good vibes from the people I'll be working closely with and how much fun will it be?

4. What's the budget, length of shoot and risk factor in getting paid in a timely fashion?

5. How's the food and accommodation being managed, especially when filming out of town?

6. Now that I know these things, what are the benefits to me? How do I feel about it?

The hero checklist means you'll be able to gauge if this job is worth your time and how you feel about it. Since your time is money, you can see how much of your time a project's going to take. How many times have you been in a situation where you say, "That took way longer than it was supposed to"? When your time is properly managed on a project, that will happen less. What's nice about it is you can decide who and what you'll give more of your time to, especially if you're going to *give it away*. And give it away without regret. Sometimes helping others can be better than a paycheck. Sound cheesy, maybe, until it starts happening to you and you see how it really helps people. The reason is, when you grow, guess what, everyone else grows with you, and the ones that don't grow, really stand out or fade away.

People see you growing, they see your perspective's changed, but not everyone can grow with you.

IT'S IMPORTANT TO KEEP IN MIND THAT NOT EVERYONE IS CAPABLE OF MEETING YOU WHERE YOU'RE AT IN YOUR LIFE.

Certain friends and family will come and go, and that's ok. It means you're on the right track; keep going.

So often I've seen filmmakers communicate in great detail for days about the story, the shots, how fun it's going to be. When it comes to the budget, that conversation is often somewhat embarrassing, very short and a little deflating.

It can seem like every conversation about budgets in the freelance world goes something like, "We don't have a lot of money. This is a really low-budget thing, we're pulling lots of favors." I got to the point where I just starting telling clients, "I'm glad you told me that, because the last project I had, they just wanted to spends tons of money and didn't want any favors." It's a funny truth that usually gets a laugh. If it was a union production from a studio, that might actually be true.

It reminds me of a big network show I have a friend on. He mentioned to me that they rented a large stadium here in Los Angeles for around $125,000 per day for several days. It was $75,000 per day for prep and wrap-out days. The studio only shot there for two of the four booked days due to scheduling issues. Seems crazy, yet to a $100 million dollar production, it's the agonizing cost of doing business to forge ahead. They may have also have been insured depending on the exact reason for the scheduling issue. The story gets even more interesting. I learned that they weren't even using the playing field in any of the shots. They simply rented the building for its architectural style and were using other parts of the stadium, but not the field.

DON'T LET PEOPLE TALK YOUR EAR OFF ABOUT THEIR PROJECT WITHOUT DISCUSSING THE BUDGET WITH AS MUCH CARE AND PASSION.

If your project takes place out of town or in another country, you'll want to know about accommodation and food. I can't tell you how many times over the years I didn't communicate this well up front or I didn't put it in writing. Can you guess where I ended up or what I ate?

About ten years ago, I did a feature film in Virginia. I secured a deposit and drove an RV with the director and producer, full of my camera gear and lighting, from Los Angeles to Virginia to start the film. We were there just a few days, and I learned that the so-called producer was just a bully. And the director had never directed anything. The crew was living on some cold fast food, and the loose ends of the shoot were really starting to show. No one was in control, and rumors about funding were starting to decimate the project. When I communicated how the crew was feeling, I was challenged to what felt like a high school fight in the hotel room by the bully producer.

I tried to explain, "I'm not here to fight you; I'm just telling you how the crew is feeling." They decided this was not a good alignment, and production ended up booking me a ticket back home, which was fine with me.

The next day I was on a plane back to Los Angeles with 16 camera bags. I had oversized road cases, which the airline charged $100 each for. Production realized at the airport they didn't have enough to cover the ticket and the bags, so I had to pay the extra $1,600 to get the heck out of there. I would also lose around $7,500, which was the balance for filming. It was a total disaster, and I was determined to try to recoup what was owed. After all, I had a contract, and I was owed for some of my expenses and time.

When I got back, I spent more time and money going to small claims court. I hired a process server, and after several months never got a single cent. What I learned is that you can be right. You can sue someone and get a judgement against them, and get nothing. If they are worth nothing and have no assets, you get nothing. If they do have assets or have credible worth, you can spend more time and money going farther. So when people say, "You should just sue them," no, you shouldn't. You should think about the time, cost and energy it's going to take. You should think about what that does to your daily life and how it fits in. In my experience, I didn't want to chase someone and go through all that to get nothing. I didn't want to be paying attorneys hourly fees for me to try to have some sort of vengeance on these jerks. Legal battles are never fun. They always take way longer, they're expensive and they can be pretty painful.

It just wasn't the life I wanted to live. This is a hard truth about the Wild West.

The same thing applies to making the wrong choice on the wrong project; it'll take longer, be more painful to get through and you make less.

THIS IS WHY IT'S SO IMPORTANT TO USE THE HERO CHECKLIST. USE IT LIKE A CRYSTAL BALL. REMEMBER, IT'S A SUPERPOWER THAT GIVES YOU INSIGHT INTO THE FUTURE. AND IT ALLOWS YOU TO AVOID POTENTIAL DISASTER.

One of the most fun parts about filmmaking is the beginning. It's the honeymoon stage for a lot a relationships. It's too early for anything to have really gone wrong and everyone's meeting for the first time with excitement. Your cell phone battery will be challenged to its limits and you'll be swept up into the fairytale once again.

The first production meeting will be the first of several multitasking meetings where half of us will be on our phones, texting or looking into something important and gathering resources. That's just how things go on an indie production. The great news is *really great*, and the bad news is *dramatically bad*, and there is no other news. You might hear things like, we're getting the funding for our film, we might be getting it, we got it, we lost it. We're going to start next week, we're pushing till next month, actually we're on hold now.

In the Wild West, things are wild. There're a lot of gunslingers in the room. The environment is often volatile and can change at any moment. This is where we start to build trust or lose it. This is where uncertainty is king and where creativity thrives. The excitement can be intoxicating.

Welcome to Wild West.

CHAPTER 2
SO, YOU WANT TO BE A DIRECTOR?

Most of the new filmmakers I meet want to be a director. There's an allure to directing, and while many people will not claim the leadership aspect of it, they will stake big claims in the creative part. But you can't have one without the other.

The first definition of a filmmaker on Google says:

*A **filmmaker**, or film director, is someone who is in charge of making, leading, and developing movie productions. It is a career that allows an individual to use their leadership as well as creative thinking skills to lead and direct major motion pictures or made-for-television films. -careerexplorer.com*

Notice that the word *lead* was used three times and *creativity* was used only once. I've been a wingman for countless directors that had zero leadership skills, sometimes even minimal technical ability and communication skills. What I mean by this is you can be the greatest creative artist ever, but if you don't know how to lead people, it's going to be a nightmare. And maybe not to you, but to them, or worse, to the entire group.

ALL EYES AND EARS ARE ON YOU ALL DAY, SO HOW YOU ACT AND REACT COUNTS AND IS BEING NOTED.

Get ready to be the hero and the villain, sometimes multiple times a day. You'll be built up only to be torn down and then built up again. And then you won't be needed until they say they need you again.

Sadly, this is the truth, and most real working directors will concur. It's not everyone's experience, and there're always a few lucky lotto winners, but like a big jackpot, it's rare. The good news is now you know the truth and can prepare. This preparation is essential to your balance of creative wealth and creative health. I want to congratulate you once again because this is a major milestone. It may be tough to hear some of these truths, but I don't want you to end up finding out when you're in the middle of your project.

HAVE A CLEAR UNDERSTANDING OF HOW TO LEAD. THAT'S THE FOUNDATION OF REAL DIRECTING.

What kinds of qualities does a great director possess? It's certainly not the tired, old stereotype of the chubby, bearded guy yelling at people. It's not the crazy prima donna that always gets their way while striking fear into the hearts of others. These are not the people that I want to spend 16 hours a day with for weeks on location. As you've been seeing, no matter who you are, the old ways of Hollywood are changing. We're not going to carry that old negative perspective anymore, and it's getting better because of you. Because you are the future of Hollywood. So what are the qualities that make a great director today?

10 QUALITIES OF A GREAT DIRECTOR TODAY:

★ Excellent leadership skills

★ Great communication and collaboration skills

★ A good listener

★ A deep understanding of time & money

★ Strong knowledge and skill in postproduction

16

★ Being solution-based

★ Unique storytelling abilities

★ Inspiring and enthusiastic

★ Humble and approachable

★ Fun

I was doing a commercial for a beauty product, and I remember the director and host having some big challenges. In fact, it was so bad that we stopped shooting for a couple hours just to pick up the pieces and try to start again. The crew was spread out all over this mansion we had rented as a location. For them it was a nice break—there was a beautiful pool and a view. I knew that the production was hemorrhaging money and the project was in danger of failing. I wandered back to the master bathroom to console the host, who asked if I could direct the rest of the day. After her spirits were lifted, I found the director in another room holding his head and sulking in misery. After hearing his sorrows, I offered this, "You know, this little ten-thousand-dollar commercial is just a workout compared to the fifty-million-dollar movies you want to direct." He looked at me and I continued, "I mean let's face it, if we can't get through this, there's no way we can handle a fifty-million-dollar film project, right? This is nothing, we can do this; we have to do this to get to the bigger projects." It was like a curse had been lifted. And with that, we went back to begin again.

BE READY FOR WHAT COMES WITH YOUR DREAMS.

It was 2007, and I had just finished another pitch meeting with a distributor that specialized in direct-to-cable movies. They were sometimes cheesy and would often air on networks like Showtime and Cinemax. I was in my thirties and had been bitten by the directing bug, so it was a dream come true. And if I didn't like a project, I'd just change my name, or ghost-direct. I cared more about the money than having my name on it. I had overhead and a business to run. The fact that I was going to be paid to write a story of my choice and be turned loose with about a quarter of a million dollars was beyond thrilling. It took a few weeks just to get the contracts signed and for the money to be in the bank, making the project *real*. This was just one of several movies I'd get to make, if I did a good job. So a lot was at stake.

The funny thing about directing is that I quickly realized I'm living in a world where I only have so much time for a given scenario. And everyone I meet and everywhere I go was going to costs thousands of dollars per hour. I hadn't even got to direct, yet.

After many weeks of preproduction, I flew the team to Hawaii, where we would shoot for about three weeks. It was easy to convince the producers to shoot in Hawaii because they wanted *high production value*. They also got to come and supervise. The reality of directing was about to hit, in a hard way. In Hawaii, the weather changes quickly. So the gear and the crew needed to be prepared. I had insured about a half million dollars of cameras and lenses, but it came with big deductibles. One minute it can be sunny, the next minute you can have a big cloud that changes exposure four stops in the middle of a take. Rain can occur at any moment, and high winds were common. While the idea of shooting in Hawaii sounds wonderful, environmentally, it has its challenges. The scenery is beautiful and did offer big production value. But that was just the beginning. I had booked a luxury mansion to be used as a location and also as a base camp. It had its own private beach and was a secret celebrity retreat. We paid $50,000 for ten days. When we arrived, I was told there had been a mix-up and there was to be no filming at the house. The property manager who greeted me on site said, "We can't let you film here, sorry. There are features of this property that make it unique, and if you show those in a movie, it's not a secret celebrity retreat anymore." Production had paid thousands of dollars to the location scout and it was his job to handle this matter, but it was beyond his ability to save it. Meanwhile, we all continued to unpack while I pleaded with the manager. "Look, I can shoot this so we'll never know where it's at!" I told him. "I'll stay in close-ups and throw the background out of focus!" I was determined, and thank God, he agreed to let us do our thing with those conditions. Naturally, many of the shots showed the whole damn house, and the neighbors complained multiple times.

But we were already rooted in, the money was in the bank and there were only a few days left by that point.

On another day, I rented a mountainside with hundreds of gorgeous acres where there would be a horseback riding scene. I found out on the day that the actress riding the horse was terrified of horses and was reluctant to get on. I had two horse trainers at $110 an hour standing by, and I had just a few hours to get the shots I needed. Right after that, I had a helicopter coming to do another scene at $1,500 per hour. I was able to connect the horse trainers and the actress to get to a level of comfort where we could shoot. As long as the horse didn't run, we were fine.

When you direct, you are putting people in an environment that you have to consider all the risks in. Everyone is different; we have different fears and we're built differently. One time I filmed an action scene in Hollywood where there was no permit at the location. We were in a back alley behind some apartments. In the scene, a group of guys in a classic convertible get hijacked by men in masks with guns. This was crazy, typical indie filmmaking. "Wait a minute!" I said. "The people in the apartments don't know we're filming! And when they see the guns they're going to freak out!" The very young assistant director told me, "They're fake guns, and they'll see the cameras. We're in Hollywood." I was thinking, *did he really just say that?* "Where is the director? I'd like to talk to him," I asked. "He's on the phone." I took the call and I explained why this was ridiculous and unsafe. He assured me it was just a couple shots and we'd be fine. "Well, where are you? When will you be here?" I asked.

It turns out, he was in jail. He gave me a good pep talk. "I only have a few minutes and need you to direct the scene, Ron!" I couldn't help but say to him, "You're telling me it will be fine... From JAIL!" As much as I'd like to blame the fact that we were young and dumb or broke, fearless filmmakers, this was just asking for it. Yet, somehow we pulled it off. We did let the people in the apartments know, we kept the noise down and we were fast. I can't say that this was a proud moment; I don't brag about it, but I did learn a lot from it. I would never recommend it or do it again. It would be one of many questionable situations I would encounter while directing or being a DP. If you're willing to take on the accountability and responsibility of directing, you can certainly own it for the well-being of your cast and crew.

The important thing to understand about money is that it's all relevant whether you have $25,000 or $25 million. There's generally never enough time or money, no matter the budget. The fears and concerns that come with that have a similar emotional impact. We'll talk more about this in the "Time & Money" chapter.

Directing is like being in a band. You can't do it without the other members of the team. You'll spend more time traveling, doing interviews, meetings, rehearsals and prep than you will playing live on stage. That's directing too, think about the amount of time you'll actually get to direct. Depending on *your* definition of directing, it can be a lot or a little. It shines a different light on the job when you consider it and look at it for what it really is.

How many times will you give it a pass and say something like "well, that's just the business." No, that's you allowing it, and keeping it alive, again.

WHEN YOU STOP MAKING EXCUSES ABOUT THE DREAM OF DIRECTING, IT BECOMES EASIER TO UNDERSTAND WHAT IT REALLY IS.

It's a choice you should carefully consider. In my experience, you never stop leading. You'll lead your entire team as well as people you don't know that may not even speak your language. You'll find a way to communicate with young people, old people, even animals; your touch will be on everything. You'll be leading in unknown territory, often. Create a safe environment so that everyone can do their craft as joyfully as possible. You'll see it in the finished product. And when you take care of your team, guess what, your team takes care of you to the tenth power. I cannot do the level of quality I want on screen without my team. They help make it possible, and without them, it just wouldn't be fun. So consider your crew and how they'll be fed and sheltered. Give them good food so they can give you a solid day's work. I've told many productions, "Please don't feed us pizza or junk food." I give them the why behind it and a better alternative that's within the same price range. It's not expensive to eat healthy when you have done the proper prep.

Great directing considers everyone and everything. After all, that's what you're in charge of.

In the old days, the studios would ask directors in pitch meetings, "What can you bring this in for?" What they meant is, what's it going to cost to get the film made? When they made a production deal, the payments were staggered, based on completion goals.

Because even the studios knew way back then that the big risk was *getting it finished*.

It's ok to admit why you want *control*. Maybe you've had some bad experiences where you wished you were *in control*. Or, maybe you know the story and characters so well, you have to be *in control*. Whatever your reasons, it's important to know that even the best directors are not fully *in control*. We're going to talk about that in great detail in the upcoming chapters.

BY PROVIDING A GREAT JOURNEY AND A GREAT FINAL PRODUCT, YOU'LL GET LOTS OF WORK.

One of the big challenges, especially for new directors, is getting work. The simple truth is, when you provide a great journey and a great final product, you'll get lots of work.

If you're looking to be in charge of a multimillion-dollar project, you have to be able to ask yourself some hard questions, just like a studio may ask. But it's also important for you to know where you're at. And this is the way to do that. Write down your answers and read them later or the next day. Modify your answers and really think about how the "network, or the studio, or the client" hears and sees you.

Earlier, we talked about setting intention, being of service and establishing trust. That's the starting point to getting the check signed faster.

HERE'RE SOME THINGS YOU WANT TO ASK YOURSELF AND EXPLORE. WRITE DOWN YOUR ANSWERS.

What kind of projects have you done? What celebrities have you worked with?

You've never directed a film or a project like this. Why should we hire you?

What does it feel like to go to work every day? Are you stressed? Excited? In control? How's your free time?

Whom do you surround yourself with to support your mission? Are they helpful? Is anyone holding you back or in your way?

How do you handle conflict? Do you get stuck or hung up a lot on what people say?

Do you brag about what a great multitasker you are? Or do you need 100% of your focus on one thing at a time?

Would you direct a project with someone who wants to fund the project, and star in it, and do many other jobs on it as well?

How do you handle intimidation when important circumstances are at stake?

What's this project going to do for people?

Don't worry if you don't have all the answers. And don't worry if you read some of your answers and cringe a little. These are some hard questions.

Like many of the things I'll teach you, it's more about preparing. It's about knowing yourself and where you're at with the details. This helps minimize finding out in the moment when there's pressure and time and money at stake. When you know your boundaries and what you stand for it'll help you navigate everything better.

THREE THINGS EVERY DIRECTOR OR TEAM LEADER NEEDS TO KNOW.

#1 BE A GREAT COMMUNICATOR.

People are generally quick to answer, "I'm a good communicator!" Great directing means you've got to be better than average on this.

How you do this is through the words you use, your tone and final delivery. Remember, everyone's watching and listening to you all day, every day. Good days, bad days everyone will witness how you handle it and lead them through it, or not. Most people don't really recognize the power of what I'm talking about. They're quick to brush it off and rule the way they want. But the truth is, this is another superpower.

I've experienced directors that are terrible communicators for decades. They rely on other department heads to do it for them. They have a deadline, fires to put out; they can't be bothered with worrying about their tone or how the words they use affect people.

This is where some of the questions we talked about earlier come into play again. You have probably witnessed some bad leadership yourself.

Imagine what it feels like to go to work every day *as that person.*

Whom are they surrounding themselves with, and is their horrible leadership trickling down to the department heads, and eventually the crew?

The answer is yes, of course it is. It's like a drop of poison in a clean glass of water—it changes everything.

What's the solution?

Be a great communicator. Choose your words carefully; think before speaking; *think* before reacting.

Always keep in mind that you are the leader! When Moses led the people through the desert, they bitched and moaned about everything. It's too hot. There's not enough food. How much farther? Is this really going to work?

Making movies is a similar process. Imagine if Moses would have gotten fed up halfway through the journey and become a reactor or a victim instead of remaining a leader. Chances are, everything would have changed and nobody would have made it.

Treat your team with respect and be approachable and clear. Remind everyone to have fun and watch out for each other. Put important details in writing for reference and share them. When you do this, it makes going to work a dream. You'll look forward to your new alliances and friendships.

You've made people feel safe; you've supported them as artists. And guess what, your project will likely be more fun and turn out better than you imagined.

#2 MAKE TIME AND MONEY YOUR FRIENDS.

I was excited to be in the same room with Bradley Cooper, Lady Gaga and Sam Elliot for a private screening of *A Star is Born*. After the show, they were taking questions and talking about what the experience was like.

PEOPLE MAY FORGET A FILM, BUT THEY NEVER FORGET WHAT THEY WENT THROUGH MAKING IT.

At one point, when describing the journey, Bradley mentioned, "We just didn't have the time or money to do that, so we had to do it this way...." For a split second, the amateur filmmaker in me thought, *You didn't have enough money* on that show! I quickly regained my thoughts because I knew that time and money didn't care what film it was or who was in charge.

Here's the big learn: it affects everyone and everything, no matter who or what. When you have more of it, it just means there's *more of everything*. The stress a director feels from a ten-thousand-dollar commercial is similar to the stress on a ten-million-dollar film. Stress is stress, more or less, it's stress and it's all relevant. What I mean is when you have a deeper understanding of time and money, it's very much the same situation and emotion.

It doesn't matter how expensive something is or how you only need another ten minutes if you've got a deadline. Why? Because a deadline is a deadline, whether it's a ten-thousand- or ten-million-dollar deadline. If you're saying, "But ten million dollars! I would treat that differently." Really? Why would you? You'd just be creating extra stress and intensity for everyone because there's *more* at stake and you're afraid. As a professional, it shouldn't matter what the budget is; you should be bringing your best anyway. Stay away from creating extra stress and drama because there's *more* at stake. You're going to do amazing work with a crew of 5 people or a crew of 50 people. That's why people hire you. They know no matter the scale or intensity of the project, you're going to consistently deliver great leadership and results. And when your client sees that you and your team are less affected by stress on bigger projects, you get more projects.

When you hire the right department heads, like your producers and assistant directors, it insulates and protects you as a director. This way you can build the proper plan that will be your map to success.

THE 3X RULE.

Buffer, buffer, buffer. I call it the "Three Times Rule."

The biggest thing I've learned about time and money is plan on it taking two to three times longer and being two to three times more money. Why? Because eventually, in films, that's what always happens, just like Bradley Cooper mentioned.

You might be thinking, *that's no way to run a business; I can't do that.* Actually what's worse is if you don't do that. You risk getting a version of the script, not the actual movie you wanted, and that's if you finish on time. The reason why is you didn't use the 3x Rule. I've told productions, "If we stick to the plan, the worst that can happen is you'll have time and money left over." When does that ever happen? You might have heard this referred to as E&O Insurance, or Errors and Omissions. And it can be a hefty portion of the budget with big deductibles. The 3x Rule is a little different.

The 3x Rule applies to many things, not just movies. It applies to remolding houses, building custom cars and almost anything that involves creativity. Why? Because creativity is uncertain. There's an unknown that we won't know about until we're there and in it. The best way to start is to schedule, budget and create a great map to success. Try the 3x Rule and see if it helps alleviate some stress about time and money planning.

The 3x Rule will also show you if the time and money you're spending make sense, because you'll be able to see how much value they're bringing, or not.

GAG: A JOKE OR AN AMUSING STORY OR SCENE.

I recently did a meeting with a visual effects supervisor and my production team. A visual effects supervisor oversees the digital effects during filming and through the post process. I'm going to refer to it as VFX, for short. I brought in the VFX supervisor before we began filming to get an idea of the time and money. This way we could properly write and plan all the VFX sequences accurately. It's really easy for an independent film to spend up to $20,000 a day or more doing unique VFX. But what it allowed me to do was weigh out the amount of screen time a VFX gag would play and how valuable that gag was. So, as an example, we had two $10,000 VFX gags that were getting quite a bit of screen time. But we also had six more VFX gags that were only $1,000 each and were on screen for just a few seconds each. It was a great way for me to evaluate why it made sense for the production to spend $10,000 on a single VFX gag. These were some of the hard questions I had to ask myself, just like you did earlier.

Rather than the producers and investors ask me, I explained to them why it made sense. I suggested that we spend $10,000 on the two big VFX gags in the film and about $6,000 on several smaller gags.

The reasons were simple: it's going to get good screen time and deliver a high entertainment value. It will likely end up in the trailer and/or the marketing materials. It had such a big "wow factor" that it was worth it. It would also be supported with the smaller, cheaper VFX gags to keep the audience under the magic spell of storytelling. It also gave the VFX team more money to amortize the way they wanted on more than just two VFX gags. Which meant we had more VFX and more production value.

WHAT MAKES PRODUCTION VALUE?

Preproduction meetings are the best. I know a lot of independent projects say we don't have time or money for preproduction. But in some way, they end up doing what they can. Remember, preproduction is where you can plan on how to save money and be the most efficient, so if you skip that part, you'll be missing out. That means you'll probably be figuring it out on production time, *in the moment.* Some situations may call for this.

I was hired as the director of photography on one feature film, and I was planning out what kind of gear we would need. Rather than just submit an expensive wish list of gear, I would explain *why* and what the costs would be. Sitting across from me was the executive producer. "Why do you need this expensive zoom lens?" he asked. The lens was a 45–250mm ARRI ALURA. It was about $35,000 to buy it at the time, and I wanted to rent it. I explained that our A camera (that's our main camera) would live on this lens for the life of the shoot. I also mentioned we would not have to stop and change lenses on this camera ever. He asked me, "How long does it take to change a lens?" "Just a few minutes," I replied. He had more questions. "And how many times do you generally change lenses in a day?" Hard questions, but I was ready.

Together we determined that in a six-day week, we spent about four hours changing lenses on our camera if we used primes. By getting the zoom, we didn't have to change lenses and gained about a third of a day per week back. We were gaining time now and could keep shooting. It was also important to note that many of the shots were filming animals. The zoom allowed us to instantly be where we needed the frame to be and not miss an important moment.

At this point he was happy to spend the extra money because he understood *the why* behind it. And after several weeks, we had gained more than 12 hours back just from that one decision. It was like getting a free day back in the schedule. Everything you do is going to come back to time and money.

Remember the 3x Rule. Try it. You'll be glad you did. Whatever something costs, plan on it costing two to three times more. You'll be less frustrated and actually get what's on the page, not a version of it.

#3 HAVE A DEEP UNDERSTANDING OF THE POSTPRODUCTION PROCESS AND ITS RESOURCES.

Postproduction is *at least* the other 50% of the filmmaking process. It's also the only thing that can save your scene or movie from technical difficulties and more. Having a deep understanding of these tools can make or break a film's ability to be convincing, engaging and entertaining. It can also save a film that wasn't properly shot.

Sadly, many films run out of money by the time they get to postproduction. Usually it's due to poor communication and an improper use of time and money. Another way to say it would be bad leadership.

Postproduction can painfully extend the length of a film's completion. It can be expensive, and I've even seen projects held hostage in post.

Why does this happen so much?

There're a lot of reasons, but in my experience it's because the leadership didn't have down the three things every director needs to know. The fault almost always lies in communication, time, money or a combination. If you're having lots of "ah ha!" moments while reading this, that's good. Because my intention of teaching you these things is to accelerate your directing skills and keep you working, that is if you still want to be a director. There's some key areas you need to study and learn as much as you can in. Now I'm not saying you have to know everything. But when you have an understanding of the whole process, you're going to be worlds ahead.

As an example, I love 3D modeling; it fascinates me. But I know it's a whole thing, it's a career, a whole world of evolving information that goes really deep. What I do is watch some highlight reels and tutorials. I look at the 3D model libraries and see what's available and how it articulates. I familiarize myself with the resources. Some of the best 3D and VFX works are the stuff you never notice. Sky replacements or removing objects is priceless in postproduction.

Knowing postproduction is a superpower.

THE MOST IMPORTANT TOOLS IN POSTPRODUCTION.

★ EDITING

★ SOUND

★ MUSIC AND SOUND DESIGN

★ VFX

★ COLOR

Remember, you'll still be directing your post team.

I'm going to give you some bullet points on why these are so important.

Editing: This is where the story comes together. Timing is everything here. This is where you find the flow of your story.

Sound: Pro sound is essential. People will forgive a bad, out-of-focus shot, but not bad sound. Bad sound will take an audience right out of the scene.

Music and Sound Design: Music makes great stories. It's the backbone of movies. Sound design helps nudge the audience's emotions. And when properly sound mixed by a professional they truly make the success of a great film.

VFX: We see visual effects overused all the time. We've seen some really bad cartoon-like VFX also. Depending on your story, genre and budget, you can use VFX to get that "wow factor!" That will make your project unique and stand apart from others.

VFX can add big production Value and secretly repair and enhance scenes.

Color: When you think of color, you may think color correction. But color goes much farther than that and is a powerful tool that's often underestimated. Not only can color correct but it can create looks or moods by warming or cooling the overall look and feel. In horror movies it's used to make the feeling uncomfortable or sickly. It can draw the eye *to* something, or *away from* it. It can be used for skin smoothing, a powerful resource I use in many of my projects.

BY HAVING THIS KNOWLEDGE OF POSTPRODUCTION, IT WILL EASE YOUR STRESS AND STRENGTHEN YOUR ABILITIES WHILE DIRECTING.

Even though we've talked about some of the horrors of directing, it actually can be a joy. I can honestly tell you the flip side is great. There's nothing like waking up and going to work with a group of artists that feels like family. Together you share a bond and you have a freedom that doesn't come with any other kind of job. It's in those times that nobody wants the project to end because they love it so much. It's the reason when the production does end, people are often sad to leave and hope to work together again. This is where you meet your film family. Be a leader that your team can be proud of and look up to. Not just on set, but in life as well.

When you do these things, you'll find great joy in your work. Distractions are minimized, and the flow is less chaotic or interrupted. You'll be less stressed about money. Because the truth is, you love it so much, you'd do it for free if you could.

CHAPTER 3
EGO AND THE ADDICTION TO FEAR

Let's be honest, people love being safely afraid, and they're willing to pay for it. Rollercoasters, horror movies, escape rooms — fear is in demand. I thought about opening this chapter with a dramatic story. Before I do that, I'd like to say something positive about ego. Most times, egos get a bad rap because they're usually associated with something negative. So before I burst into several stories about how I have experienced plenty of negative egos, I'll share this little tale where my ego got tested *to the fullest*.

I was in Beverly Hills, filming with one of the hottest actors in Hollywood. It was a familiar scenario; I was told how much time we have the actor for and what we needed to get. We had the healthy amount of shots in a condensed amount of time. I had two brand-new hard drives with way more storage and backup than we needed.

When you're with celebrities, everything goes into fast forward. Meaning, everything is happening faster. It's because their time is valuable and they're only willing to give so much of it. We're going to be doing the same *with our time*. And we'll dive deep into it in the next chapter, "Time & Money."

If you want it to be a smooth, efficient shoot day, make sure you really have everything ready when the celebrity arrives. On this shoot, there was going to be a fair amount of improvisation. So we didn't know exactly what might happen. *Uncertainty*, there it is again, how can I plan for that? I also had limited power because the hotel was very old and we were up high, so a generator was not possible. We were in a 1,500-square-foot presidential suite. I had strategized what kind of wattage my lights would be, but we blew the breaker anyway. *Funny,* I thought, *for a huge elite room with a near-$10,000-a-day price tag.* Everyone uses lots of power when a movie crew shows up. Makeup and hair can use one hair dryer that could take up to 1,500 watts. I've seen curtains catch on fire from overloaded circuits or hot lights. So these are things that are always on my radar. Anyway.

The crew was hustling hard and we were on the last shot when one of my team came up to me and said, "We're having a problem with the hard drives." I was of course concerned, but not scared. But I was also in the middle of the last hustle and bustle setup that we'd been doing all day. So there wasn't a lot I could do in that moment *anyway.* My ego assured me that I had plenty of media in the cameras to finish the rest of the day. I didn't need to stop and deal with this now. I also knew that the team was dealing with this in the background already. As soon as the last shot was done, I thanked the celebrity actor who was gracious and incredibly talented. Then I made it a point to get back to the data transfer area and see what was going on with the hard drives. The person that manages all of our digital media from the cameras is called a DIT, that stands for Digital Imaging Technician. They are responsible for making sure everything we record in the camera gets onto a hard drive and also gets backed up. I found my DIT in tears and a couple other team members troubleshooting. "The hard drives are not mounting! We know all the information is on there, we saw it, everything was fine. We've tried other computers, we've tried everything." I reassured the DIT that we're going to figure this out and that it was not their fault. I knew we had two brand-new hard drives that were quality drives. I also knew that I never experienced this before. How could two brand-new hard drives all of a sudden stop becoming recognizable to the computer, especially since they were working fine all day? And this is something I've done hundreds of times before. It sounds silly, but for a moment I felt like Captain Kirk from the original Star Trek. I told the crew, "You guys keep working on this and let me know when you get us back online." I had to talk to the producer and make them aware of the situation we were dealing with *in the moment*. The rest of the crew was wrapping, taking pictures and high-fiving what a great shoot it'd been. Meanwhile, in the next room, there's a technical tragedy going on that only a few of us knew about.

I found the producer, and I calmly explained the situation, "We're having an issue with the drives. They stopped mounting on the desktop and we're trying to figure out why." "What are we going to tell the director?" she asked. And like Captain Kirk, I said, "We're going to tell him the truth because we've never dealt with anything like this before." Then fear started to set in. What if we lost all the footage! Again, ego assured me we would somehow *be fine*. Deep down, I knew that we had shot so much incredible improv. I thought to myself, *there's no way this was not going to make it out into the world*. Now I had to convince a very stern director of that.

The producer and I met with the director in a private area. And I explained very calmly about the situation. It was both unusual and uncommon that two brand-new hard drives would suddenly stop working right before we're done. There was no one to really to blame; it seemed like it was the equipment. I also offered a solution that I believed in. I did explain that the material we shot was magical. I expressed how I felt it was meant to be out in the world and somehow we were going to find a solution. I knew that there was some data recovery software I could experiment with, but I didn't know how good it was and how long it was going to take. The director actually took it really well and just asked to be updated as we found out solutions.

That night I tried some data recovery software, but no luck. I went out on my balcony and I asked the angels for their help. Then an idea came to me. I thought about asking one of our relatives for help.

It was a bit of a long shot because it was late, and he was always busy and traveling the world fixing computer systems. But he actually answered right away and I was able to bring the drives to him early the next morning. He was able to run it through some high-level recovery software and recover all of the files. Everyone was beyond thankful and relieved. Later, the producer confirmed with me, "Hey, Ron, the only reason I was calm and didn't freak out *was because you didn't.*" It was a great trust-building moment for sure. That same producer and I became close friends and work with some of the world's biggest celebrities today. While my faith helped put me at ease, my ego played a big part in keeping me confident that a solution would be found quickly.

Ego can give you strength when you need it the most. Courage doesn't have to be cocky, and confidence doesn't need attitude. Like everything, there's a light side and shadow side to it, so it depends on how you use it and how you let it use you.

YOUR EGO HAS AN INSATIABLE APPETITE. IT'S ALWAYS HUNGRY FOR MORE.

Your ego is going to get in the way all the time. It wants to lead you. One of the most impactful quotes that I'll never forget was when my soulmate, Frankie, gave me her brief definition about the shadow side of ego. She explained it like this: "Death to the self before death to ego. It wants to be in control. It wants to look good and feel good while being front and center. And, it wants its way all the time. In a very sad and extreme example, ego can convince the mind to end one's life. Otherwise known as suicide."

DEATH TO THE SELF BEFORE DEATH TO EGO

This is one of my favorite and most powerful descriptions of ego, by author and teacher Deepak Chopra:

"The Ego, however, is not who you really are. The ego is your self-image; it is your social mask; it is the role you are playing. Your social mask thrives on approval. It wants control, and it is sustained by power, because it lives in fear."

That's a description that really got me thinking. Too many of us are addicted to fear. There's a massive adrenaline rush that comes with involving yourself in a lot of risk or high demands. And when you pull through and accomplish or exceed your goal, it's a satisfying rush and your ego wants to repeat it again and again.

Filmmaking always creates interesting challenges for the ego. I had just got to set to film two actors in two different videos when I noticed the producer *notice me*. I walked over. "Good morning," I said with a smile. Then I got the news. "So listen, we have two actors that don't like each other. They can never see each other or cross paths today." As ridiculous as it sounds, I knew she was serious. So we designed the whole day around that in order to keep the peace.

Fear can take you out of a situation fast. Ego can get you into a situation fast-er. Ego and fear are a team; they work together and they work fast. That's why it's important to know them both well. That way you can recognize them working for you, or against you, in your daily life.

Something I see all the time is the fear of *lack of work, especially when that's how you make a living as an independent artist.*

Something I've always encouraged people to really understand is; what looks and sounds really cool to you may not look and sound really cool to others. No matter how cool a shot looks, if the person that paid for it, or stars in it, isn't feeling what you're feeling, you have a situation. It means the ego is concerned about something. This is where collaboration and trust go to work once again.

I've talked with many people about projects that they're very attached to, not just emotionally but also financially. Projects that are already done in fact. And some of them may have been done for a long time and are still awaiting a sale. I've learned that these are very sensitive subjects. Offering suggestions or any kind of friendly counsel can be touchy. I've had people leave the restaurant in the middle of a meeting because they were offended. I would even go as far as saying they were insulted at a suggestion, or a fact that needed to be looked at. If a project is struggling, many times creatives will become defensive, shut down or flee, especially when they're the person who funded it and put in all the hard work. I've also come to know that not everybody has a way with words and communication.

I try as much as possible to make sure my clients feel comfortable working with me. Because I establish a trust and a safe environment, it's easier to talk about creative differences or concerns. I've made it a real practice to not take things so personally. It definitely is a daily practice and I'm not perfect at it, and you may not be either, and that's OK. The fact that you're aware of it and you're doing your best every day is what counts.

Actors have roles that they play. They get into character and train with a certain mindset to become a believable portrayal. The rest of the crew should do the same in their positions. Get into your role, be of service, be your best at your area of expertise. This is not the time to brag about how in the eighth grade the teacher put on your report card, *doesn't play well with others.* If you're still carrying that, please let it go. We want benefits, not liabilities.

I thrive working with artists, musicians and performers. I want to teach you an awareness that you might already know about, but you might not be using it to your benefit.

Here's a practice you can do anytime, anywhere. I use this before meetings, before I get to set or if I'm feeling stressed.

DAILY PRACTICE

FEEL BETTER IN 3 STEPS

Filmmakers are adventurers; they're creative athletes. They take on projects and situations with a higher risk. The goals are to win, stay alive and do their best. They all use a similar technique to focus and realign when preparing for a big event. If you're a Star Wars fan, think of it like "using the force." Here's a daily technique that works really well for me. Feel free to modify it to your liking.

1: Ask your ego to step aside for a moment. Sometimes the ego has no awareness; it usually just wants to be heard and mow down any opposition. It runs on fear. You're going to put that on hold. The reason is that when you're realigning, your ego is usually first to answer the call. The good news is, you're in control; just put ego on pause and move along. Put your focus on taking at least five to ten minutes of uninterrupted time to yourself. Go longer if you can. Turn off the phone and any distractions. If it sounds like I'm setting you up for a mini meditation, I am. This is the part where you get to take a moment just for you because you can, and the results are worth it. Everyone has five to ten minutes two to three times a day to do this. And you can do it anywhere. Don't worry, everything will survive for the five to ten minutes you're away. This is really great when you're traveling and you can take even more time.

Here's what you need to do once you're comfortable. Put on some light music if you want, or just close your eyes wherever you're at and focus. Let all the problems and whatever is going on in the background fade away. I want you to think about the first three things that come to mind that you're really grateful for. Spend a moment with those thoughts and explore why you're grateful.

GRATITUDE AND FEAR CANNOT SHARE THE SAME SPACE.

2: Don't be a reactor. It's ok, you'll be allowed to take a moment to process. You can actually think about what you're going to say before you say it. The upside to this is you'll have fewer possible regrets about speaking without thinking. Don't use the tired, old excuse, *well, they said this, so I had to tell them.* Save your energy, get off the hamster wheel. I'm not saying don't get mad; I get frustrated all the time. But I've learned to be a lot *less frustrated.* Getting worked up uses a lot of energy and time. It changes things and shows you in a very different light to everyone around you. Remember, if you're a leader, everyone's watching and listening *to your lead.*

3: Let go of stress. Ask yourself how much of this stress or drama you are creating. A lot of times we'll paint a picture in our minds that is far worse than reality. Be careful you're not getting high on fear—it's addicting. Some people believe they need drama in their life; they even say it's a motivator. The trick is controlling it and balancing it. Now that you know how to recognize it, you can take your power back. And you can invest that energy where it will do some good.

It's pretty cool to know that you actually have real superpowers! Those are three steps you can take to quickly raise your awareness and see where you need to grow and realign. When you find some areas that need work, write them down or make an audio note in your device. And let's make this a regular practice. I like to keep my voice memo (or dictation) app open on my phone. That way, no matter where I'm at, when I have an idea, or something to remember, it's easy to just record it. You can now have an organized log of your notes and ideas recorded easily. As you grow, you'll be able to listen to your own notes, thoughts and feelings. And as you find the answers, you'll have even more questions, which is good. Question everything; you'll get what you want *faster*.

Let me just say right now, it's ok to not know everything. I know sometimes it may feel like we have to have an answer for everything ASAP, but we don't. Life isn't a game show where you get like three seconds to answer, and if you don't, there's a horrible buzzer that sounds. It's ok to give yourself pause and think it through. It's shocking how many times I've reacted and regretted it, only to go back and explain it all over again, the way I meant to say it. I could have just taken pause and put the right thought and focus on what I was going to say the first time.

Our minds are often living way in the future and multitasking our energies in so many directions. When a person or decision comes along, it's never really met with 100% of you because 95% of you is in other areas multitasking. That's why when you meet someone that really listens to you, it's appreciated so much. When you have 100% focus, you'll likely reach the goal *faster*.

FEAR CAN DELAY YOUR DREAMS.

My biggest childhood fear was public speaking. As a kid, I would get so nervous, I would physically shake. I didn't like reading aloud in class either. I devised all kinds of ways to avoid speeches. I would excuse myself to go to the restroom when it was my turn. But I quickly ran out of ways to escape public speaking, and finally, I had to face it.

It was Mrs. Henky, my sixth-grade drama teacher, that showed me *the ways of the force, through acting.* Somehow, it was ok for me to go up in front of the class as someone else. If I was acting like a goofball or playing a character, I felt totally comfortable getting up in front of people. My 11-year-old ego was trying to tell me something and I was listening.

At the time, my favorite actor was Harrison Ford. So I would just say to myself, *how would Harrison Ford do it?* I ended up getting a B+ on my speech, and the teacher congratulated me that it was actually the most fun and interesting of all the speeches. This 11-year-old boy had just conquered one of his first major fears.

The funny thing is, I still get nervous about public speaking as an adult. But many of the mentors and actors that I look up to have assured me this is totally normal. Once you settle into it and you keep going, you're fine. Not always easy, but true.

EVERYTHING ALWAYS WORKS OUT.
YOU'VE NEVER NOT MADE IT.

Hollywood is a fear-based environment. It's a breeding ground of egos that are fueled by fear. It's an ever-changing popularity contest on the highest level. Here're some important things to keep in mind.

FEAR FACTS & RESOURCES

★ Use fear as a motivator.

★ Get comfortable with the unknown.

★ Remember, creativity thrives in uncertainty.

★ Use your superpowers.

★ Failure is just a test to see if you're willing to grow.

★ Fear calls attention to, and demands action from, the ego.

★ Protect yourself; don't bet against yourself.

★ See yourself on the other side of the fear.

★ Carefully look at what your choices are saying. What are they saying you need validation from? And how often?

★ What are you doing to feed fear?

★ How can you do better?

I remember the first time people started introducing me as their Mentor. It made me feel grateful and blessed that people trusted me and I was able to help them. I was traveling in circles that were not exactly soft, warm and fuzzy people. They also had a lot at stake. So for them to feel this way about me was really special.

A common introduction would be something like "I'd like you to meet my friend Ron. He's a director, an amazing cinematographer, a colorist, he writes, edits, he's super talented." It feels good to hear this kind of validation. And it was true. Yet, after 30 years of being in filmmaking, I'm still learning.

My ego was happy with that introduction as well. When I started meeting people who had strange introductions, it was a bit of a red flag. "I'd like you to meet Chuck. He's a great guy but sometimes he can get a little cranky and break things after a few drinks." I'm sorry, I do not want to meet Chuck. I don't even wanna be around anybody like that, let alone make a movie with them. If I bring Chuck to an environment with a major celebrity and he decides to throw a fit, how does that make me look, especially if I introduced him as a team member of mine? My clients know whomever I bring with me on set, they don't have to worry about. And because they trust me, they trust my crew, even if they've never met them before. Look at who's in your circle. How do you introduce them and do they come with any disclaimers?

Most of us are somewhat aware that we have an ego and when it gets in the way. We find ourselves bragging about it. We even warn people about our ego and how it will set just about anyone straight. Our egos are sensitive to tone. How you say things and the choices of words you use. That's why so many of us love comedy, because it explores beyond the boundaries *in a funny way*, on purpose and *you expect it to.*

Ego and fear will run amok if you allow it. It's up to you to control it. Design the boundaries that bring you the most benefits, and keep it simple.

Ego and fear are open 24/7; they never close. I have several clients that have expressed to me the desperate need to keep shooting content to constantly feed to social media. Even though it's fun, it becomes stressful sometimes. There's a lot of pressure for an individual to have to learn how to look and sound their best. And then please hundreds of thousands of people on social media as a daily practice. It's a personal choice for everybody to decide how much of their lives they're willing to dedicate to this. Most actors and models have convinced themselves that *you have to do it*, and *you have to do as much as you can, and you have to just keep putting it out there.* When put that way, it already sounds exhausting and stressful. It's important to have some kind of strategy that works with less stress, more fun and happy results. So how do we do that?

One of the first things you want to do is be aware of how much fun you're having? Remember, question everything. How much time am I spending with this and what are the benefits? When we're honest, and we think about the amount of time and energy this kind of thing takes, the profits are usually embarrassing. I'm still talking about the constant need to produce content and feed it to the world until something big happens. It's more than a full-time job, and who can afford a publicist? Having someone else do it is expensive, and you've probably not seen the benefits there either. I've heard scenarios like this many times. Keep questioning it. Are these real benefits to me or are they social media myths costing too much time and money? If you feel like you're on the hamster wheel, rethink your plan or make the necessary adjustments. And why am I spending so much time looking to everyone else?

I was invited to a party and my friend told me, "There's going to be all of these big people there." What I realized is, it's usually the same people looking for work and networking with other people also looking for work. And everybody's looking for money because no one there has enough of it. Do you subliminally think that you're going to meet that person at the event that just wants to invest in your movie? That does happen but usually after you've made a project that's turned a good profit. Maybe it's just about the adventure of the hunt? The ego loves this attention. It's important to gauge how much time you allocate to parties and events for the chance meetings and networking. If you start to calculate how much time you spend planning, preparing, attending and recovering from parties, you might be a little surprised. This is a pivotal point where you can decide if it is a lifestyle or a business. Or is it a lifestyle business? And what's the shelf life? Imagine a business manager asking you, "When can we see the financial results of that?" It's so easy to get swept up in the fun and make excuses based on what you've heard. Be careful you don't lose months or years. If it's not really benefiting you, then your time can be better strategized. I know that sounds harsh. But I'm here to deliver a message of truth, and this is a truth that I surely know. My hope is that you spend less time than I did *learning it*. Because now *you know too*.

CHAPTER 4
THE JOURNEY OF YOUR FILM

A friend of ours had just returned from a film festival. "How was it?" I asked. She explained how every other speech the filmmakers gave talked about how they didn't have any money and it was such a long journey. "It took years to get the film made." And then she asked me the most important question. "Why do people invest in movies and how do they find money?" I enlightened her on several of the reasons that people invest in films and how they find money. When a filmmaker is personally on that journey, it has so much more meaning. That might be part of the reason that they remind everybody, when it comes to making a film, how it can be a very challenging and long road. It can also be one of the greatest joys life has to offer. And it most certainly is something you can share with everyone, and it will be here long after you're gone.

Many filmmakers don't have a clear understanding about the journey you and your project will take. Notice I said, *you and your project*.

This is the film you're going to watch repeatedly and know every detail of. You'll know all the intimate details about certain shots and why they are so amazing or not as amazing as you wished. You'll need to work at finding *the good* in really tough situations. A lot of filmmakers claim to understand this journey. I'm going to fill you in on some details you might not have considered.

THERE'RE MANY UNKNOWNS IN THE JOURNEY OF A FILM. YOU'VE GOT TO HAVE A MAP WITH A DESTINATION.

By having a map, you have a direction to go and solid a plan. A map allows you to strategize better along the way. A map is specific and contains places, dates and goals. You can call it a schedule, a call sheet, whatever it is. I think of it as a map. Even if your destination changes, you can adjust. I've worked on dozens of projects that have not had a good map or any destination. I can honestly say, without a map it's about a 99% fail rate. What I mean is there's a 99% chance that your project will not succeed. Without a map you're just guessing and throwing it out there to see if "somebody picks it up." That's ok if that's part of your plan. But not everyone feels comfortable with that kind of plan or risk. So it's a good time to explore what it's going to take to make this project come to life and be successful. The success part means it turned out better than you hoped.

Success means it made money and increased your resources. It also means your value goes up and you're likely to do it again with *more*. Success means you didn't age five years during a five-month project. It means the journey was a success too. Success means *you had fun* and you met some new members of your film family. I've met some of my closest friends on projects that we've succeeded on, together.

SUCCESS IS NOT ABOUT PERFECTION.

Successful films are built with proper tools and resources. When you limit yourself or think too small, it directly affects your film. You'll know these intimate details when you see them in editing. So be careful because you may be setting yourself up for more challenges down the road. You'll need to use proper leadership and delegate tasks with your resources. This is real directing and producing. It's what it takes to make the story come to life *the way you want*. Don't be a victim; focus and trust your talents.

Create a map so that everyone can be working together on the same page. Using online team management apps to connect people electronically is also a great tool. Or you can make your own in something like Google Docs. It allows you to give everybody a title, include contact information and dates with notes. They have live updates, so when you make a change, everybody sees it as you see it. Tell your team to check the notes online. That way you don't have to explain it to each person. This is going to save you a lot of time.

Let's take a look at what a film's journey looks like. Your project may or may not require all these steps. What I'd like you to think about first is, *what if I had all these resources?* Not, *we can't afford that; let's start cutting stuff!* Imagine if you did have what it takes to get what you want on screen. Remember, once it's done, it's out there forever *with your name on it.*

THE JOURNEY OF YOUR FILM

Here's a general example of a film's journey.

 **Contracts, pay and ownership percentages**

✪ **Script**

✪ **Preproduction**

✪ **Filming**

✪ **Editing**

✪ **Sound**

✪ **Music**

✪ **Color**

- ✪ VFX

- ✪ Submit for QC

- ✪ Trailers

- ✪ Movie poster

- ✪ Marketing: P&A

- ✪ Premiere events and festivals

- ✪ Distribution

There're about 15 steps in a film's journey. The *filming* part is just one. Each one of those steps supports the success of the project. Now imagine taking away just one of those things. Let's just say we take away color and movie posters because we're going to save money. What kind of risk are we incurring? And where does that leave us? It's so much clearer when you look at it like this.

Let's pretend for a moment that *your film* is like a car. And we say, "Hey, we can't afford the doors on that kind of car! The car will go down the road just fine with no doors." That's true, it will still go down the road. But it's not the most comfortable. It looks different, and it isn't safe or secure. So it incorporates instant risk to whoever is riding in it. Is there anything of value riding in it? "Yes, of course, there's people in it!" This is what can happen to your film when you take away resources. It can become a version of your film. The same way a car will change dramatically without doors. This is why it's so important to know this now.

Now you have a different perspective as you think about resources. Everything we decide on the film's journey affects everyone.

Remember, you're going to put everyone in the situation that is being created by you.

I know many of the films that inspired me took enormous amounts of resources. Yet, today, we can make a quality movie fast and affordably *with even better resources.* The key to success is the *right strategy.* Great leadership and trust will do the rest.

Let's take a closer look at why these resources are necessary for your project.

CONTRACTS, PAY AND OWNERSHIP PERCENTAGES

This is almost always a delicate conversation for artists. It's important that you figure this out in the beginning. Put in writing the job titles and benefits for all involved. You don't want to be figuring out who owns what when a network picks up your show and orders 13 episodes!

SCRIPT

You may already have a script or be writing one. Or maybe you're looking for a good script. Whatever the case, it's important to get the script approved. Everyone needs to agree on the details of the story. Scripts can change dramatically when actors, locations or schedules change. And things do change. This is the time to prepare for that. It's the time to develop a collaboration with your team on how flexible certain aspects of the story *are,* or *are not flexible.* Sometimes there're challenges getting exactly what's on the page. There're a few great writers whose books have been turned into movies. Even their stories don't always translate to films well. You probably can name at least one.

Make sure to include your writer as a key collaborator.

PREPRODUCTION

Preproduction is the *prep* or the *prepare* before filming begins. This is an essential part of your project's process. This is where you set your expectations and talk through the essential steps. In other words, you build the map for the journey.

The key to successful preproduction is that you're doing it. If you don't do any prep, then you're on production time, in the middle of filming, trying to figure it out. That means a slower pace and added stress. Having said that, sometimes you don't have a choice. In those cases, the risk is higher because there's only so much time to get what's needed that day. You can alleviate some stress by asking for pictures of the location prior to arrival. You can also check the weather and inform department heads where power and staging areas are located ahead of time.

There's so much you can and should prepare for during your film's journey. The DP and post team need to design a solid post workflow. If you're doing VFX, include your VFX supervisor in preproduction—it will save you money and frustration. Art directors are the life blood of storytelling and you'll want to include them now. When you hear people say, "We weren't on the same page," they literally were not. This is where everyone gets on the same page as the script.

Preproduction is the foundation of your film's journey. Make it a priceless part of your process; you'll be glad you did.

FILMING

You could say the most fun part of making a film is the *filming part*. Most people that have made good films *with bad experiences* are still glad they did. Filming *is the fun part* and it's also the work part, especially for the crew, who's always laboring. I think about the grips and electricians that carry heavy loads in the heat and the cold. To me, it's a beauty that only comes with filmmaking. Maybe because when we unite, we create something out of nothing, *and magic happens.* That's probably why I've heard so many people though the years say, "I love being on set."

EDITING

Editing is your biggest superpower. It may seem intimidating, technical and boring, or expensive. It can be all of those things. But it can also be, *and is,* one of the most exciting and powerful parts of your project's journey.

People frequently ask me, "I need a good editor! You know a good editor?" The editor is at the heart of your storytelling power. The ability to manipulate *just about anything* to better serve the story is the essence of editing. It's the place you'll spend the most time mulling over your masterpiece.

SOUND

As I've mentioned before, people will forgive a bad, out-of-focus shot, but they'll never forgive bad sound. Bad sound will take a person right out of the story. It can be one of the most frustrating parts of filmmaking, especially when you have to wait for a plane or the loud leaf blower that's blowing your shot.

The right sound engineer will be able to consistently advise you of the quality of sound they're getting daily. It makes it easier to decide when to not hold up the show and fix the sound in post or wait so there're no issues down the road. *Luckily, you have a map* so you can plan accordingly.

MUSIC

Sound and music are at least 50% of your storytelling super-powers and your film's process. Music can make or break a project. Yet, I have noticed how it is often not given the proper attention early in the process. When I hear things like "We got a guy, he's a musician. We're going to get him to do *all the music*," or "We're just going to throw in some stock music, that's all we can afford," it makes me wonder why come this far and then decide that *that way*?

Music should be an early adoption. Pick songs that represent the feeling of the scene. Pick famous songs that your composer can use to get a sense of the vibe you're going for. Some of the best music isn't much musically at all; it's a tone that supports an emotion that's aligned with the story.

COLOR

One of the most overlooked and underrated resources is color. There's so much you can do with color correction, color grading, shifting the focus, beautifying skin tones and more.

Color is one of my favorite parts of filmmaking. It's where you see your images come to life. Color is where moods are enhanced and looks are created. Dark shots are saved and weird skin tones are balanced out. You're in control, and everything looks better after color.

VFX

Visual effects are a key resource that makes a project unique. They can add massive amounts of production value. VFX can be used to remove objects or logos. You can also add objects like trees and cars or add elements like rain and atmosphere. You can do just about anything with proper planning.

I've filmed epic landscape shots when the sky wasn't cloudy or as textured as I had hoped. Or maybe the schedule doesn't permit you to be in that perfect hour for shooting. With VFX, we added the sky we wanted in post, which looked better than what was shot on the day. Nobody could tell, and it was an affordable solution.

SUBMIT FOR QC

All films must pass a quality control process known as QC. This is done before a show can air on broadcast TV and most major streaming platforms.

What is QC? It's where your project is analyzed for color and audio levels as well as any other glitches or technical problems. If any issues are found, the project is rejected until the corrections are made and then it can be resubmitted. There is a fee that can range from $500 to $1,500 on average, but it depends on a few factors, like runtime. Companies do charge a fee every time your project goes through the process. So you want to make sure you do everything you can to make sure it's technically as perfect as possible before submitting it.

This is why hiring the proper post team counts. When you combine that with a solid post workflow, you'll have little worry about.

TRAILERS

Trailers and teasers are the first thing people will see before they see the movie. These are some of the best moments condensed into a format that attracts audiences to a film. Trailers are powerful and necessary to spread the good word about your film. There can be several versions of your trailers. Your film's trailer should be engaging and leave people wanting more. It's also one of the best places to end with a *call to action*. This is the perfect opportunity to invite people to come to a website, join a group, get exclusives and more. It's a valuable tool that can build a fan base quickly or make a distribution sale in minutes.

MOVIE POSTER

Like the trailer, the movie poster is the first thing people will see before they see the movie. It's the visual representation of your story in a poster.

There was a time when you would choose a movie or even music solely based on the cover art. While it may seem like an old concept, it still works and can make you lots of money, so don't underestimate it. Keep in mind your movie poster may get seen before the trailer. This is where you convince and intrigue people to watch through artwork and taglines.

MARKETING: P&A

Prints and ads are expensive. We know that studios spend hundreds of millions promoting their films through marketing. Knowing that, what are you doing for your film? Proper marketing influences people to care about your film enough to pay to see it.

Beware if you're hearing things like "Oh, that's out of my hands, who knows?" or "We can barely afford to make the film, forget about advertising it." Then, there's the ol' "We're going to market it ourselves. We know some big people." Without proper marketing, your film will not reach the masses. And if you're leaving it up to the distributor, you should ask how much that's going to cost and check their marketing abilities. It will come out of the film's profits, and sometimes these fees can be shockingly high, especially if it involves film festivals and events. Distributors will often only charge you a fraction of what it would cost to take your project to the film festival yourself. But the reason is that they have 10 or 20 other films similar to yours that are sharing the cost. So when they attend a festival, it's not just for your film, it's also the 19 other films they may be representing there. Think about all the films that are streaming and in theaters right now and how they let audiences know where and when to go see them. Think about how you start hearing about them months before they're even available. How else would the world know?

Marketing allows you to test the waters by using focus groups. This way you can test the success of your film and advertising before spending loads of money in ad spots. It also tells you what's working and what isn't rather than you having to guess or claim to know. Be prepared for feedback, use it to your advantage, strategize with it. You need people that are not as close to the project as you are to give you their feedback. This is your audience. When you know your audience, you'll be a big step ahead of everyone.

PREMIERE EVENTS AND FESTIVALS

Events and festivals are a great way to spread the word about your film. Inviting people to a fun festive event and showing off your film can be a joy. It connects you to people in magical ways. Seeing a film on the big screen in a theater is its own unique experience. It's better in every sense because there's an audience and it's larger than life. This is the definition of the movie-going experience. It's something we all look forward to that reunites us again. We celebrate it with our film family and share it with the world. And in that moment, *we're all* on the same journey.

DISTRIBUTION

Some films have distribution secured before they even start filming. Others are on a quest for distributors once they have a cut of the film. And some distribute their films themselves.

If your film has a certain popular actor attached, you could acquire distribution before you start. Wherever you are in this, eventually your film's destination will be some form of distribution. Many people have told me they would never film anything without a distribution deal in place.

Here's an example of a common situation with distributors. When you consider the side of the distributor, it's a bit of a different perspective. Imagine someone bringing you a film to sell. "Who's in it?" you ask. "Nobody, no stars. But we've got some really talented people. And it's a great story." It's now your job to convince people to buy it. But the last person that brought you a film said the same thing. In fact, you've got a whole roster of movies similar to this competing. Some have B- and C-list actors, and some have no recognizable names. Some have great posters and trailers, and some are trying too hard. It's a little easier to see when you consider the distributor this way. They usually have several films that are in need of making a profit, and the faster the better. Take a look at their library and see how your film fits in.

This should give you a really good perspective on the journey of your film. When you decide to make a movie, there's a big process behind that commitment. Make sure you develop a clear, strategic workflow and explain it to your team. When someone offers up a strange plan that goes completely off course, it's now easier to see why the fail rate is so high. You'll recognize the added risk and it's easier to see *the real benefits* as well.

Give yourself strategic access to the resources you need to make your film the best it can be. People have often told me, "We just don't have the money to do it the way the studios do. We're a low-budget film." Yet, your project will be competing with all those movies and more. It's at that point that you may want to have a better plan. Or consider waiting until you can get more funding to make the movie the way it should be made. So many times I've seen people fall under the curse of making *a version of their project* just because they're anxious to make a film, and they jump at just about any option. Use the 3x Rule—you'll be happy you did. The worst that can happen is you'll end up with more time and leftover money. And a film that's even better than the one you intended on making.

No matter what, consider the journey of your film because it's taking you with it.

CHAPTER 5
TIME & MONEY

Most people know that *time is money*, but they're working with limited knowledge of how to positively apply that in their lives. Let's be honest, if you are aware of time and money and you're not using it to the fullest potential, *what are you doing?* Let's take a look at some of the challenges you might be facing.

As entrepreneurs, we all have a creative side and a business side. But our inner creative side and our business side don't always get along. In fact, they clash most of the time. Why? Usually because the creative artist wants to have fun and play. Artists like to spend time together creating, collaborating and goofing off. I've come up with some of my best material laughing and goofing off. It's probably the reason that I love my job so much. Who wouldn't want to go to work doing that?

The business side of us sees us goofing off and asks how much money that's putting in the bank? The business side understands that there's overhead, deadlines and responsibilities. It's constantly monitoring the benefits, growth and value of what we're doing. It can be frustrating when we're reminded that *it's time to get to work*. The business side also knows that it takes a lot of money to stay out there doing what we love. It's expensive to live in the big city; healthy food is expensive. In fact, everything seems like it's on a *cost clock*. What's a *cost clock*? I've always pictured it as the virtual timer that we're all on wherever we're at. But it reminds me of the little meter at the gas station pump. Depending on how hard you squeeze the handle, the numbers go really fast. It's especially like that in movies. That's why they cost so much. The next time you're watching a movie, imagine a *cost clock* at the bottom of the screen. See if you can guess how much money has been spent during certain scenes. It's actually kind of a fun game to play, but it can also annoy people that are not in the movie business. Keep in mind, the moment we get on set, the *cost clock* starts running.

So how do we get the creative side to play well with the business side? We can't have one without the other, and we need both to be working together to really succeed.

The first step is to get your inner artist to understand that the business side is there to support you. And without it, you will likely not succeed, or may get taken advantage of. When you have a better understanding of where you're making the most money and why, your artist will go get *more of that.*

PROFITS ARE A BYPRODUCT OF YOU DOING AN AMAZING JOB AS AN ARTIST AND ENTREPRENEUR.

The creative side needs to pay close attention to the details provided by the business side. This could be schedules, budgets or just common sense. The true intention of your business side is to protect your artist and keep you out there doing what you love. The business side needs to be gentle with our inner artist because we are fragile. Don't take this as a sign of weakness just because we can be fragile or delicate. It's because we're sensitive or empathic as artists. This is a deep inner relationship, and when these archetypes come together, you can do just about anything. They live inside you; they're not in anyone else's head or heart. It's powered by your spirit, that's why it's an inside job. Get these archetypes on the same page working together and they'll take you farther than you've ever been. If you want to have some fun and gain a deeper understanding of how archetypes work, check out the Disney–Pixar movie *Inside Out*.

I've worked on so many independent films and projects that don't have a business side. Or the business side is weak and is overrun by artists trying to figure it out. This makes my business side very nervous about a few things—some of the things that we've already discussed. Like getting paid, how's the food going to be, will it be a fun shoot or a nightmare? When there's little to no business side in charge, the risk goes way up. When I encounter this, I recommend people that can help, like a producer, production manager or an assistant director. They can help get the production on track with a map, which lowers the risk for everyone. I remind these productions that they're going to need somebody strong in this position for it to be a good journey and great result. Remember, it's about getting what's on the page, not a version of your movie. The business side will help accomplish this. I've seen large productions held up and messed up over a $2 missing prop or countless other silly reasons. There'll be questions about "Where are we at with this, how much did that cost, what time do we have to be out of there?" And it'll all be happening in the chaos of production so you'll need somebody that has accurate answers at any moment. Do not make the mistake of trying to handle this while directing. Unless you want to be more frustrated and direct less. Position your key people as a buffer to protect you so that you can keep directing, or whatever it is that you do best.

THE BUSINESS SIDE OF FILMMAKING SAYS DO THIS THIS WAY AND GET THIS RESULT.

Things don't always work out the way we have them on a schedule. No problem, that's where our creative artist thrives. The business side operates with a different intuition than the creative side because we're looking at different things for different reasons. As I go through the journey of each project, I'm constantly weighing out visual benefits, cost, schedule and risks. In other words, time and money.

New technology always comes at a premium. But sometimes it's worth paying that premium to get the advantage. LED lighting has been such a joy to work with. Not having to lug around giant heavy lights and generators has made independent filmmaking a little easier when it comes to lighting. In fact, it's made it so easy that many people have joined in on the fun with limited lighting knowledge. Now you can stand back with your phone or an iPad and adjust all the lights and color temperatures with instant results. The lights are lighter, take less power and don't get hot. I've had several incidents where I've set the lights and somebody has gone along and changed it during shooting. I would tell the crew, "Don't touch the lights. I've got them set for skin tones." How does this happen, you ask.

AT TIMES, INDEPENDENT FILMS CAN BE LIKE WRANGLING KITTENS ON THE PLAYGROUND.

I can see why certain directors of photography seemed like such jerks when it came to laying down the law on set. They were probably just sick of people not listening so they had to flex some power in a memorable way. I have had to set these boundaries too. Sometimes certain people will only listen when it's delivered with a certain strength and tone. I've had a couple of projects come back to me in post and say, "What happened to the skin tones in the shot, can we fix it in color?" The translation is it's going to cost more time and money. Which is why it's important to not only listen to the person in charge but have someone you trust in charge. A great leader explains the boundaries of the environment they bring their crew to. It's essential to communicate things like "Don't touch the lights" or

"We've created some markers. Please stay within this area for the best lighting." There's a very clear reason why we set up gear a certain way and why those instructions need to be followed. I've seen lots of people go rogue over the years and wind up hurting themselves or others. Remember, it's a team, and what you do will affect the team and the result.

In 2010, the RED camera was one of the first 4K digital cinema cameras that had successfully shot movies that were shown in the theaters. Most people were still shooting film and were incredibly skeptical of digital. Like anything new in technology, it had its pluses and minuses. But I believed so strongly that digital was here to stay that I actually took some of my savings and invested in a RED camera. I found a used camera with less than 100 hours of use and saved about $5,000. For the next year and a half, I would be more of a technical advisor than a cinematographer, most of the time explaining the benefits of shooting digital. Calming people's fears and addressing their concerns was something I had to do before I even got the job as a DP. Nobody really understood the workflow, and it was just too new for a lot of people. When it comes to business, Hollywood likes familiar and low risk. By default, filmmakers tend to doubt the unfamiliar. Imagine being one of the first productions to say, "We shot on digital, not film."

In the meantime, I had just spent a grip of cash and made a bet on a technology that the world might not have been ready for yet.

I had gotten a call from Professor Nate Thomas at California State Northridge College, otherwise known as CSUN. He had a project that he was shooting with his students and wanted to introduce them to shooting it digitally on the RED camera. It was a series of public service announcements (PSAs), and the client was the FBI. They wanted some educational videos that included cyber bullying and awareness about illegal child labor. I got to introduce everyone to digital cinema and its benefits. I helped them get familiar with the camera settings and develop a workflow. Most of all, I made it fun and showed them there was nothing to be afraid of. It was a great shoot and a wonderful first experience for everyone filming digitally. Those PSAs would go on to win an Emmy Award. I was now starting to see confirmation that I made the right choice. It had nothing to do with my not liking film; I actually love film. It had everything to do with a new resource, and a new medium that was available for us as artists. It allowed us to do our jobs more efficiently and affordably. What I ultimately learned was that this was an example of the business side and creative side working successfully together. It worked so well, the group won an Emmy Award that we never expected. Many of those students I ended up hiring on several productions of my own.

INVESTING IN PRODUCTION EQUIPMENT

Somebody was showing off to me their new camera system. It was well over $20,000 and had a nice overall build. In my head, I was doing the math on how many times they would have to rent that out just to break even. This is a very common thought process that everyone goes through when considering investing in equipment. But what you think, and *what actually happens*, is usually different. So is it good to invest in gear or should you just rent?

The best investments come with gear that's working often. When gear is sitting, it's not making any money and the new models are coming out. The market is also becoming much more saturated with cheap rentals competing for business. So it makes sense to invest if you've got a project that's long enough, or consistent enough, work. At this point, there's so much gear available for so cheap that it doesn't make sense for me to buy a super high-end setup. I love renting, because everyone's competing for my business. I've got a great selection of equipment, and when people ask me, "What kind of gear do you have?" I tell them the truth, I have access to everything affordably. I can honestly tell them I can get whatever is right for their budget.

DON'T FALL FOR THE OLD MYTH OF
"YOU'VE GOTTA OWN EVERYTHING."

That may make sense if you're going to be in production for many months or you've just signed a Netflix deal for thirteen episodes. Renting means that if there's an issue with the gear, you can usually get a backup pretty easily. The rental companies are there to support you and they usually have multiple pieces of gear. Your equipment insurance will allow you to be covered if a rental is faulty, or costs you time and money. If you own it, you have to get it in service and then go get a replacement while in the middle of production. For me, the biggest downside to renting is the hassle factor of picking up and dropping off. Here's a tip to help alleviate that.

I charge a small fee within the rental cost for the pickup and return. So, as an example, if I'm going to rent a nice director's monitor and it costs $60 a day to rent, I'll charge $100. The $20 fee to pick up and another $20 fee to drop off after the shoot is beyond reasonable. That's just one item. When you start renting multiple items and charging those fees, guess what, you make more money. If production wants to have somebody handle the pickup and deliveries, that's great. That just means you've gained time. And since time is money, you'll be using that to your benefit.

Don't be fooled by thinking, *we need to hire somebody that owns all their own gear*. That can be a big mistake. You're hiring somebody for their skill and talent, not what they own. I've seen camera crews show up with a truck full of expensive equipment, and if there's a disagreement, away they go, holding the production hostage. When you rent, and things aren't working out with a crew member, it's easier to replace that person and plug in the new person and the gear stays on set. After all, the show must go on, *right?*

I'm going to let you in on a big secret that's going to put money in your pocket. Productions are perfectly OK with renting some extra equipment if you don't own it. It's a myth that you should only hire people that own all the gear *that might be needed*, especially when it comes to high-ticket items like cameras and lighting. When you're hired for your skill and talent, productions will listen to your advice about renting gear. Look at that, there's *trust* working its magic once again.

Productions are usually OK spending money renting the necessary gear when you educate them as to why and what the benefits are. And when they rent, *you make money*, bonus money. There is work involved because you'll be answering lots of questions and coordinating the rental houses plus the pickups and deliveries. So this is not some tactic on how to pull one over on production and make extra money; there is work involved. But you're working with their money, not yours. On top of that, technology and equipment are changing so fast. And we all know this, when you buy a camera, there's already a new one coming out in just a short time that's better. Camera companies are in business to sell cameras. And the market is more saturated than ever with production equipment that's available to anyone. I use camera companies as an example because they're amongst the most popular investments. Consider this: Do you think the camera companies make more money selling the really expensive high-end cinema cameras or the cheaper, prosumer 4k and 6k cameras? They make more money when they sell *more*. This is another example of business and creative coming together.

When new technology comes out, particularly in the camera and lighting world; a lot of people want to get their hands on it. When you can be the first person to shoot with the brand-new camera that's popular, it gives you an exclusive edge. It gives you bragging rights that are exciting to potential clients. Since I've owned several of the very first RED cameras to hit the market, I can really speak to this well. After a year or so of educating people on what a cool camera it is, the RED became in high demand. But not everyone could get them quick enough, and I already had one so I was working pretty steadily. But was it a good investment?

The answer is both yes and no. Because it took a couple of years and depending on how you look at investments, that could be a long investment. Remember I spent the first year or so educating people. I was preaching the good word of digital cinema. I got lots of heat from the old crotchety cinematographers that were set in their ways. But largely, the people that focused and listened, they adapted with the technology. They were open and put in the time, which turned into a very positive result. Studios started to quickly convert to digital cameras. People were finally starting to embrace the workflow and how to operate them correctly. Digital cameras are new technology, so they don't always work perfectly. Or they're finicky when you started attaching third-party items. Speaking of third-party items, let's talk about that because that's the key to the investment.

People always ask me, "What camera should I buy?" That's the number one question I get all the time. I tell them that they should use the 3x Rule. Here's how it works when it comes to cameras. Whatever you spend on the camera body, multiply that times two or three and that's what you need to invest to have a great camera package. When you add accessories like extra batteries, a monitor, a tripod, bags or how about a camera stabilizer?? It's very easy to spend way more on what you'll attach to the camera than the camera itself. So remember, you're not just buying a camera, you're buying a camera package. Even if you don't buy it all right now, it's important to consider. I know plenty of people that just want to own a certain camera body with basic accessories and they rent everything else. Keep in mind, there's faster than ever turnover in equipment. But there're a few key items that will last a long time that are solid investments. What I recommend is buying key accessories that will work on just about any camera body. That way you can use multiple camera bodies and be more flexible for your clients. Not to mention, it's a smart investment strategy. You can design an accessory package that may include a good monitor, tripod, gimbal or lens set. Build one that works for you right now, and for the future. A good set of lenses can be used on multiple cameras for a long time and can be a great investment.

Just because it seems like you're needing to rent a camera all the time doesn't mean you need to buy one for $15,000. If you live in an area where there's just not a lot of access to high-end cinema cameras or production gear, then it could be a reason to buy if the demand is there. But it's important to make sure that you're going to be able to put this piece of equipment to work as much as possible. If you've already made the financial commitment to a nice camera package, you've already decided. Congratulations, let's go!

THE 10 BEST CAMERA ACCESSORIES TO INVEST IN

1. ON-CAMERA MONITOR

2. FAST MEDIA

3. WIRELESS VIDEO

4. LENSES

5. TRIPOD OR STABILIZER

6. LAV OR BOOM MIC

7. SLIDER

8. CASES OR BAGS

9. VARIABLE ND FILTER

10. LED LIGHTS

THE BARE MINIMUM CREW

Productions often ask, what's the bare minimum crew that you need? Here's a list of key people that I recommend. This is a general crew list for camera and lighting departments. It can be accessorized and modified in a lot of ways, and it's a great starting point.

★ Director of Photography (DP)

★ Assistant Camera/Focus (AC)

★ Gaffer (Lighting)

★ Grip (Rigging)

★ Sound

It's easy to spend $5,000 to $7,000 a day on camera, lighting and sound. That's just on these few people and some gear. Can you do it for less? Sure. What are we giving up to do that, and what's the risk? It's important to investigate price. Sometimes services are cheap for a reason and you find out later.

Make friends with time and money. Notice when they're in your favor. And even when it's not in your favor, you should be asking "why?" Think about some of your big successes. Think about the steps it took to get to there. When you're mapping out your future goals, look at the steps you believe it's going to take to get to them. Write them down and check them off as you achieve them. This is a key part in the map of success.

The skill and talent that you bring is unique. That increases your value, and it also means you only have so much time to allocate to each project. The way I'm describing it kind of sounds like you're a celebrity. Well, guess what, *you are*. Your time is valuable and so are *you*. Whatever money you might be lacking can be fixed by implementing some of the things we've already discussed. You've used your time wisely just by reading this. Now think about the actions you're going to take to go higher. Make a map and see the steps. It's in these moments that time *truly is on your side.*

CHAPTER 6
WHY YOU'RE LOSING MONEY

Many of the people I have worked with that are new to film-making are trying to figure out where they fit in. I wonder why a lot of them start with directing. Could it be they have a story they want told their way? In other words, "I want to be in charge. I want to assume all the risk and responsibility. I want it done *my way*." Ok, great. Don't be afraid to ask what that pays. Look at how you feel going through the process. Is it tormenting and are you telling the "war stories" from the set again and again? When you look at all these things you can manage them better. Be honest with yourself and you'll never go wrong.

I know what it's like worrying about bills. I've assumed all the risk that comes with the rewards and faced bankruptcy. At times, I've felt like there're only a few people left I can count on. And my rich friends were nowhere to be found. Life becomes more challenging when you're building a profitable career and carrying financial stress. Things will happen that you didn't plan on. Let's take a closer look at some of the reasons you might be losing money.

What's the most frustrating thing about doing freelance work? This is the question I've asked in several large filmmaking communities. Sixty percent said getting paid.

As a freelance filmmaker, it's really easy to get overwhelmed with just a couple of jobs. If you get two or three jobs requiring a lot of your time, you start feeling that intensity, and maybe some stress. And I know it seems like everybody calls right around the same time, right? But there's only one of you and there's only so much time in the day. Nobody wants to really turn down work, especially if they could really use the money.

As artists we have to be careful about how much time we dedicate to one client or project. Because chances are another one is right around the corner. And by using some of the practices that we've already discussed, it'll make it easier for you to take on multiple projects. I'm not talking about multitasking; I'm talking about changing mindsets. You'll need to be able to successfully get in the mindset for each project. And you owe it to that project because they all require something a little different. I've sometimes gone from a scary movie to a comedy the next day. You may already have multiple projects that you want to do that include all kinds of different genres. Make sure you take the time to get into character.

Independent films usually start with little money and little time. As the production continues, the idea and the resources grow, but the budget doesn't. So it's important to really keep that in check. Watch out if your project is evolving into this great *bigger deal* but you're *still* working with the same budget.

WHAT YOU'RE RISKING IS GETTING A VERSION OF WHAT'S IN THE SCRIPT.

That means you might have to make compromises or last-minute adjustments based on whatever hand you're dealt at that moment. So just because you have access to a lot of great resources doesn't mean you should use them. It means you still have the same budget and the same schedule to stay on track with. Once you start adding to your resources, it likely will add to your timeline, and it usually adds to your budget too. This is another big reason why the 3x Rule really works.

Watch out for these costly time and money traps:

★ Too many meetings

★ Favors

★ Discussing *too much creative* before talking about the budget

★ Free preproduction and no preproduction

★ Having one big client that disappears

★ Fees that you get stuck with like parking, meals and transportation expenses

★ Longer days than originally agreed to

★ The waiting period after wrap to actually get paid

★ Adding more jobs to the job you agreed to

★ We can only get "it" on this day or at "this place"

★ People that too frequently "run late" or need to reschedule

These are all things that can cost you dearly if you're not really on top of it. And if you're doing a job that doesn't have a lot of profit margin, it may end up costing you money to do the job. That's why it's always a good idea to have a production agreement stating exactly what you're going to do and what you're not going to do. You may have to refer to it when more is being asked of you. And even though productions will often cry about their situation and try to make you feel guilty for not helping, you already have an agreement. This is not the time to take advantage of anybody and squeeze money out of them. That would be the wrong thing to do. It's time to talk about what you can do to help and what's reasonable for everybody. Sometimes there is no logic or reason to the demands of a production. But the truth is it's not your burden, so don't take on production's burdens. Most productions will keep asking and asking and asking of you, if you allow it. Please do not let these extra demands start to pile up on you and your department. I've heard countless filmmakers complain like victims about how production is in a situation and they're trying to help them. They know they're not obligated but they're bitter about it. It's a personal choice that we all have to make. And every production usually winds up in distress one way or another. If you really want to help them, then really help them. Be careful not to be the victim throughout the process. I've rescued hundreds of productions through the years and sometimes I didn't even know why. I suppose because it was based on a feeling and a process. And most of the time that feeling was right on the money, literally. I would always make a connection that would lead to friendships, more work and more money.

I came across a YouTube video recently that explained the process for lottery winners after they've won hundreds of millions of dollars. Life changes and all kinds of people start to discover you if you don't use the proper process and protect yourself. What I found is, a lot of people don't realize when they come into money if they get too flashy they can become a target. I'm not trying to freak you out; it's just another important point of awareness that you should know. If you're driving expensive cars and showing off the insides of your house to the whole world, everyone kind of knows where all your stuff is. It sucks to have to say this, but that exposes you to some potential high risk. When people become fans, some of them will do anything to be close to you, or at least know where you hang out. I've known countless beautiful actresses that have gotten a number of odd requests from all across the world. But what does this have to do with losing money?

Several things. One immediate thing I've noticed is safety and security. It affects how you conduct your daily life. Celebrities and wealthy people have a lot at risk, and limited time. There're a lot of people that want to get to them. Hiring a security service is often the safest, most efficient choice. Depending on your fame factor, getting a ride in and out of an area that you want to spend a little bit of time at can quickly become expensive. I've had countless lunches with celebrities, and we always have to allow extra time because somebody will be taking notice and interrupting. There're certain restaurants we can't go to because we just won't get anything done or it won't be safe. So there's specific places we can go to meet with a little more privacy in order to have a nice lunch and get some work done.

Since I've been in Los Angeles, I've experienced two carjackings while driving fancy cars. Both involved a high-speed escape that was not fun or anything like the movies but, instead, terrifying.

What about legal issues? When lawyers get involved, things get expensive and time goes slowly. And speaking of legal situations, they can and will use anything in your social media against you. I'm not telling you this to scare you; it's really important that you understand it's simply a choice and an awareness that you should have.

Before you begin the adventure of making a film, there're some things that you should also be aware of that could cost you more time and money.

Time and money go much faster with:

★ Company moves

★ Stunts

★ Children

★ Animals

★ VFX

★ Large groups

★ Specialty equipment, like jibs

★ Lighting

★ Makeup

★ Partnerships and favors

★ Becoming a social media slave

A lot of these things can bring great production value to your project. But it's important to be aware of how much time they can cost you if they're not properly managed. I've often asked a crew member, "How long is that going to take?" The person I'm asking will usually say something like "I just have to '*do this*' and then I'm done." The problem with that is that you don't know how much time it's going to take. And the next thing you know, more time has passed than you'd like. So now when I ask that question, I ask it like this: "I need to know how much time that's going to take *in minutes*?" I'll often get the same answer and I'll ask again, "So how long is that *in minutes*?" I'll even go as far as saying with a smile, "Is that a real five minutes or are you thinking more like a *Hollywood 10 minutes?*" This is where you can see where your time is really going. You can blame the situation, but the truth is the truth and now you know where your time went. This means that you can prepare for this type of thing. Plan on it because it happens frequently in filmmaking. And when you use techniques like the 3x Rule, you'll have a lot less to be concerned about because you'll be more than prepared.

Money-Saving Tips:

★ Use a credit card with rewards points when renting gear or charging production expenses.

★ Preproduction is where you save the most by making a map.

★ Hire film students, save a little on rates and utilize educational resources responsibly.

★ Negotiate better stage and equipment prices by booking during slower times and multiple days.

★ Delegate tasks.

★ Set time limits for everything.

★ Don't beat yourself up over "turning down work."

★ Trust the real process.

★ Negotiate all-inclusive flat rates when possible.

★ Don't commit to a schedule or budget you don't agree with.

★ Order groceries and essentials online when possible and keep working.

Using the opportunity of ordering groceries and essentials online has been one of the best practices I've implemented in my lifestyle. It's a way for me to get my time back. I can plan ahead, get exactly what I want and keep working. I can even order extra to take with me for the next day. How many times have I been in the middle of editing or writing and "ding," my food for the week showed up. It's masterful and perfect. When we're really engaged, our mind wants to keep going, but we also need to take a break and add nourishment. The time I've saved not having to go to the store, or spend even more money at a restaurant, has been monumental. And since time is money, that's like putting money in your pocket.

The people that deliver our food do an incredible job. Make sure you tip them well. And feel good about it because they are helping support your well-being. Be happy to pay the fees; it's a small price to pay. What you charge for your creative expertise is nowhere near the small premium to have food or essentials delivered directly to you.

It's times like this that it feels good to invest in yourself—*this is your lifestyle*. And it has a longer lifespan by design. It's one of the best feelings when your choices are paying off. That's what it should feel like when you're in charge.

WHAT YOU THINK AND SPEAK BECOMES REAL.

Most filmmakers will tell me, "I don't wanna turn down work." But the truth is, you can't afford to take every job because every job is not the right job for you. What we're really saying is that we're concerned about the timing of when the jobs happen. It would sure be nice if they all happened on a schedule where you could do them all. But still, are they the right job for you? Just because a job's available on a film doesn't mean it's a good job, the right job or at the right time for you. And that's what we're really looking at. We language it by saying, "I don't wanna turn down work." But it's not what we really mean; in fact, there're a lot of things that we say that we don't really mean. And that's the problem; we're carrying that language and it makes it real in our own lives—it becomes *our truth*. It's crazy when you think about it, *we* really are responsible for keeping these things alive, especially if that's the story we're telling.

THE MASTER PROCESS

I'd like to share with you a workflow I call the Master Process. The first part will help you determine if a job is right for you and you are right for it. This Master Process allows you to stop losing money and get your time back. When you use this process, it's going to get you where you want faster with less frustration and *higher profits*. And my favorite part, *you*'ll be more faithful to the script by being able to put what's on the page *on the screen*.

Pay attention to how your projects evolve when you run them through the Master Process. Your perspective may change and that's good because you'll be able to adjust while you have more time. Here's the checklist for the Master Process that all your projects should use. You might recognize some familiar parts.

THE MASTER PROCESS FOR PROJECTS

★ Interview your clients by asking all the details and specifics about the project.

★ Talk about your care, like food and housing,

★ if you're on location.

★ Do you like the script and the people? How does it feel taking this job?

★ It's good to ask questions. Aid and advise the production on anything you see lacking so there're no surprises.

★ Get all your production agreements in writing before you begin work.

★ Make sure there're clear and specific job titles assigned.

★ Producers and production managers, make sure you include this in your production agreement: Any additional rentals or additional costs of any kind will require approval. Without approval, production is not responsible for any costs.

★ Set the intention by delegating authority amongst your team members and departments. And hold people accountable.

★ If boundaries are crossed, make sure you can get support from other team members so that you're not dealing with the situation alone.

★ Be OK with not knowing everything. If you don't know, it's OK to say so.

★ Make sure that people are clear when there's an unknown factor. That way there's less shock or surprise if it becomes challenging down the road.

★ Find out who your go-to producer, or person for answers, is.

★ Know your post workflow in the beginning.

The Master Process is going to show you right away the specifics of the job, and it'll give you a good sense of the people involved. In other words, it's like a crystal ball for what you're considering getting into.

THE GUIDING VOICE OF THE ASSISTANT DIRECTOR

The real job of the assistant director is to be a guiding voice. What you say and how you say it matters here more than ever. It's your voice that the crew is going to hear that is going to guide them through everything. This means the good times and the bad times. It's important that this voice is consistent no matter what time it is. I've often been this guiding voice. It's allowed me to practice my tone and choose my words carefully. I've been in foreign lands where I've had to earn the respect of some tough crews in hard environments. And just like using the force, it works.

Remember we talked about it—people want to be led, especially by a great leader that's inspiring and enthusiastic. Some people may argue, "It's not my job to be inspiring or enthusiastic. It's my job to get the film made, no matter what." I've been on set with many of these directors and ADs. I was once under its spell too. What I found is, that mantra is never helpful or comforting in difficult shooting situations. It's like saying the crew is expendable. And production becomes this war machine rolling over the land chewing up anybody in its path at all costs. This can cause severe trauma and depression to creatives. This might've already happened to you. Or you might know somebody that this happened to. What does this have to do with losing money? It has everything to do with its victims. When filmmaking becomes a battle-field, it gets more expensive. You lose people. People are not enjoying themselves and will often stick it to you more when they can. And quite honestly, most people on jobs like that are just taking a check.

I found when you can connect with the crew and really create as artists and share that mutual respect, *magic happens*. That's why we're there anyway, remember? But we get caught up, distracted or offended.

WE GET HIGH ON PRESSURE AND BECOME VICTIMS.

When you have a solid trust with your crew and something more is needed (*like overtime*), it's usually given with more kindness at that point. When I work with somebody I like, I'm willing to really go the extra mile that much more because *I like them*. And this is true for a lot

83

of people; it's that simple. People do more business with the people they like.

Many filmmakers I know have been prisoners on film sets for weeks or months in terrible conditions. And half the time they don't get paid what they're owed. Can you believe that? That's what it has to do with losing money. So you have to watch out for these jobs that are a race to the bottom. When you use the Master Process, it will help filter out what you don't want, and it'll really highlight the jobs that are meant for you.

START HERE WHEN PLANNING A PROJECT

If you have a script or concept and you're ready to begin a project, start with these five things:

1. Set the intention of your team's journey

2. Choose your key people (Department Heads)

3. Determine your locations

4. Design a post workflow

5. Set a solid schedule and budget

When you set the intention of your team's journey, you're deciding right then if it's going to be a good journey or a terrible one. Most of the time, independent productions know that they're under-resourced. Yet they'll make the project anyway, bitter attitude and all. Watch for the signs; set a great intention before you begin.

When you choose your department heads, it's important to delegate. These are going to be your key people that you'll bring with you. These are the people that you're going to trust, and they'll be in charge.

When you determine your location, it gives you all kinds of useful information. It will test your schedule. You'll see where you can put the camera and lights. One of the most crucial things to watch for at your location is something that you won't be looking for at all. That's because it's sound. How's the sound there? Is it noisy or are there garbage trucks and airplanes? If your location is not sound-friendly, it could be a costly mistake in post. Be sure and check your locations. See how sound-friendly they really are and plan accordingly.

A solid post workflow is the *make or break* of every project. I have worked on several projects that were being edited as we're shooting them. It's so important to have your post workflow determined before you begin shooting. You'll need to know specifics like how much storage space you'll need, how long each department will need for editing, sound, visual effects and more. Similar to the way you develop the shooting schedule, you'll have a post schedule as well. If you don't have a post schedule, you'll have no clue on when your project will be finished or how much it will really cost.

As your information comes together, you'll be able to gather it and then form a budget and schedule. The budget and schedule may evolve as ideas change. It's important to remember that if ideas change and the budget never does, that could be a problem. I see a lot of independent films that start out as a small, simple idea that grows with incredible resources into a much bigger production than what was planned. This is pretty common in independent films. If your resources are great and they're growing chances are it's affecting the budget and schedule. So make sure as things evolve, the budget and the schedule agree with those details. Otherwise you may end up compromising or getting a version of what's on the page.

CHAPTER 7
BRINGING SEXY BACK

I started the very beginning of my film career as a makeup artist. I really wanted to do creatures and FX, but when I went to school I had to learn all phases of makeup. I first had to learn high fashion, then theater, then movie and prosthetics makeup.

I was always doing really cool projects. A lot of my friends were models and actors. Halloween was always a great time of year. I was very comfortable with my job. Part of the fun of doing makeup was making people *look and feel* beautiful. It was hands-on. Conversions had no boundaries. Women would often ask if I thought *they* needed a boob job. Or they would hint that they were thinking about getting one. Get two! You should do both boobs, I would jokingly tell them. But really I would tell them about makeup artistry. I would say, "You look great. If you want your boobs to look bigger, we can use highlights and shadows to shade them. Your boobs *will* look bigger in the lighting."

I was introducing the world to the self-esteem benefits makeup had to offer, not just on the face. I also worked with a lot of African-American and dark-skinned cultures. It was a known fact that a lot of makeup artists had difficulty matching dark skin tones. I always custom-mixed my foundations because sadly there just weren't as many great options in professional makeup for darker skin tones *at that time*. And this wasn't *that long ago*; we're talking the nineties. People were really frustrated, and thank God the selection is much better now!

Guys would laugh and say, "So you get paid to do makeup? Do you ever do like body makeup? How'd you get that job?" I had a lot of uncles from the deep south that would just kind of go, *"Huh... that's good son."*

I was body-painting girls like tigers and I was friends with countless centerfolds. It was my job to keep them looking and feeling sexy. One of the key things that I learned in makeup school was the importance of being a professional friend to the person sitting in my makeup chair. I mean let's face it, I knew what they looked like when they came in at 5 am. I was in their face all day, and there was a lot of intimacy and trust. I've helped actors in and out of wardrobe, sex scenes and various other vulnerable moments on and off camera. The fact that I started at 19 years old was kind of crazy, looking back. It allowed me to evolve and thrive as an entrepreneur in an environment that was particularly exciting to me.

YOUR SEXUAL ENERGY MATTERS.

I was putting myself right in the middle of a playground of sexual opportunity. So what does this mean to you? It means that *you too* are likely going to be placed in the middle of the playground of sexual opportunity. Or, you're in it now. It's a byproduct of many filmmaking environments. It's not everywhere, but *it's everywhere.*

I was able to navigate successfully by keeping work, work and sexual play and just sexual play. These were my friends, my clients and they trusted me; I couldn't betray that trust. I've heard several stories from gorgeous women, wherein men had violated that trust. Besides, I was with these clients every day for weeks at a time. This was early training for me. It was showing me that everybody needed a guide. I had been somehow placed with beautiful people because that's what I was attracted to. I know what it takes to create and maintain that beauty. The *sex part* was just a small part in the big picture. And it would take me a while *to really get that part.*

My professional relationships didn't involve sex. They often had their own unique intimacy, vulnerability, trust and fun. Sounds crazy, right? Think about it. They were so much more powerful than *just sex*. I was positively influencing people's self-esteem. The people around me didn't just look better, they felt better too. Looking back, I now know it was the universe's way of preparing me for writing this book.

Guys are pretty silly about wanting to be intimate with an attractive woman before they know her. Some guys act like they're keeping score, or that you get an award for it. Guys can be clumsy and they sometimes stumble through romance. For others, it's like a scene out of National Geographic. The real truth is, *once you really know a person*, the sex part is so much better. Otherwise, if you're having sex with strangers, it's just a chore. Sure, it just feels better than doing the dishes. And you know this because after the sex part, you come to your senses, and you don't even want to be around that person. And it's back to work.

Today, as a filmmaking coach, I am often asked by people... "How do I know if I'm looking for the right person? How do I know if I'm with the right guy or girl?" I would ask, what's the relationship like the other 85% of the time you're not having sex? You know what's interesting, even if you're some sexual dynamo, you're not going be having sex more than 15% over the course of your relationship. It's safe to say that at least 80% of your relationship is going to be about everything other than sex. How does that part feel?

IT'S IMPORTANT TO CREATE A SAFE ENVIRONMENT FOR YOUR PEOPLE.

This is true, particularly if intimate scenes are going to be happening there. Remember, you're not there for sex. You know why you're there. *In the times that I have taken the bait*, the sex has never been as good as I imagined it. Which is why it's better to just leave it to the imagination. And that's just not in life, *that's in your storytelling too.* Belligerent sex and nudity are just gratuitous and usually not necessary. Unless there's a real reason in the story as to why we need to see it. Be careful when you use it because too much of it, *or the wrong kind of it,* can quickly cheapen your project or make it overly offensive. What's really interesting is that when big celebrities do gratuitous sex scenes, it's OK. It becomes big news, almost like they planned it that way. Somehow, showing glimpses of X-rated sex is perfectly fine if the named celebrity is big enough. Isn't it funny how Hollywood picks and chooses what's OK?

What's the difference between sexy and gratuitous?

Sexy is just enough to tingle the imagination.

Gratuitous is often ugly, uncalled for and leaves little to the imagination. They're both powerful tools when used correctly. Speaking of powerful tools, let's talk about a tool kit that Hollywood uses, and abuses. I call it the *Devil's tool kit.* I use it more sparingly now, but I used it a lot in the beginning of my career. I'm not suggesting you use it, but it's something you need to know about. Hollywood *leans on it, and overuses it.* You've surely experienced it at the movies.

Here's what the Devil's tool kit consists of.

THE DEVIL'S TOOL KIT

- Sexual Situations
- Excessive Profanity
- Shock & Horror
- Evil & Corruption
- Pain & Suffering

The Devil's tool kit is surprisingly simple and streamlined. The use of just one of these items will dramatically affect your audience.

Moments in our stories require our audience to feel an impact or experience the suffering of a character or situation.

IT'S SOMETIMES THE KEY INGREDIENT IN THE RECIPE, BUT TOO MUCH CAN RUIN THE DISH.

You're going to be exploring some of these situations and emotions with your people. Which reinforces what I'm saying, be a professional friend. Don't pervert or cheapen your relationships by falling victim to the shadow side. The shadow side is always a lie. It's fleeting. It's a scam. Don't fall for it.

Making what looks dangerous on camera, *safe in person* is a skill. When you set the intention *up front,* you reach a level of comfort together and can explore that through filmmaking. I have clients that I can be extremely raunchy with, and we have a lot of fun. I have other clients that are very professional, and I never use a curse word. I do my best to make it all about them. It's their image and their voice telling the story *as a character,* playing a role.

Music videos are perfect examples of performances that use the Devil's tool kit. They're often clawing for your attention. Lack of talent is often camouflaged with techniques straight from the Devil's tool kit. Just like we talked about earlier, when you take away all of the makeup, costumes and lighting, what's left? Some of the new music videos often make me feel like I've just been at some version of a strip club. I guess I just miss real talent. What I mean by that is I've seen people sing with no makeup, in their regular clothes, with no lighting and they're incredible because they're talented. Because they have real talent, it doesn't require the crutch of all those other things. When makeup, costumes and lighting become *enhancements,* the real talent shows even more. It shines through no matter how a person looks or what their weight is. And to me, it stands out like a sore thumb when talent is overproduced, underdressed and over-lit and they spend thousands on post retouching. Even though I have a trained eye, I feel like other people know this too.

HOLLYWOOD IS WELL AWARE OF THE DEVIL'S TOOL KIT.

These tools put a lot of money in the Studio's bank accounts. They uphold these "expressive freedoms" that are powerful and impressive, especially to the young. They use these intriguing qualities to lure us to watch what they have in store. We can learn from this without making it our lifestyle. These are storytelling tools and resources. Don't get high on your own supply.

Remember, the creative relationships you'll have will sometimes be provocative and powerful. You'll make impressions on the masses. It will almost certainly be more satisfying than any sexual escapade you may have while filming.

Explore *what sexy is to you.* Are you following the rest of the sheep? Have you been programmed to believe what someone else's version of sexy is?

SEXY *STARTS INSIDE AS A MINDSET*, THEN AS A VISUAL, AND QUICKLY TRANSFORMS INTO A FEELING, ALMOST IMPERCEPTIBLY.

Let me tell you some more about what sexy is. The energy it emits is highly contagious. It's thought-provoking. It tickles the imagination while it flirts with us. It's hungry while it prowls and purrs. It takes us to a place we don't want to leave and are excited to return to. We get to play *dress up* when we're sexy. Sexy is unique to you because you're the only person that can do it your way.

SEXY CAN BE STRONG AND VULNERABLE AT THE SAME TIME.

How you use it in your life and your storytelling is up to you. Everyone connects with what sexy is in their own way. When you're working with professionals, it's important to communicate this and remove the guesswork.

What's sexy to you, *really*?

CHAPTER 8
CREATIVE HEALTH BECOMES CREATIVE WEALTH

I'm always reminding my people to take care of themselves. I remind my film family, "Be careful you don't get that ten million dollars and a health problem." It's one of those statements that makes you go, "Hmmm, right!" It's a quick way to snap out of the busy curse you're under for a quick reality check. When I encourage others, it helps encourage me too.

My mother had a unique name. Her name was Argie, and she is my biggest inspiration. I was a miracle baby. Doctors told my mom she couldn't have children, and yet, hello! here I am. My mom was not wealthy; in fact, she grew up on a farm, very poor. She wasn't even able to finish high school because working in the field picking cotton was the priority. When we hear that today, we might think, oh that's sad, or that's crazy. But the truth is, today we're doing the same thing under different circumstances. We're making stress the priority. We get addicted to it very easily without even realizing it. As I'm writing this, I see a headline that reads, "Harvard study shows 90% of doctor visits are stress related." We'll spend lots of money on "work stuff," but cheap out on ourselves when it comes to nourishment. My mom always reminded me to eat good and take care of myself, so I could be ready for a big day. What's so hard about that?

I was fortunate enough to do several feature films and television shows working with my mom. I was about 22 and I got a TV series as the key makeup artist. I needed a hairstylist, and I hired my mom. After a few weeks she would remind me, "Your father's going to think I've left him." And she was right, she had to get back to my dad who was 500 miles away. Mom would go on to open her own hair salon and get her cosmetology license at age sixty-two.

One time I handed my mom a check and she said, "I used to make 30 cents a day. Whoever thought I would make this kind of money *in big time Hollywood*?"

These are treasured moments to me; they are absolutely priceless. And I was so grateful that I could have those experiences. That's just one of the areas to find riches in creativity. When you do a good job doing what you love, a nice paycheck becomes the byproduct.

Movies are powerful; you'll become a part of everyone's journey. The magic is in the people we work with. I've gotten big jobs from the production assistant who was sweeping the floor two years ago and is now directing a feature. Everyone is important, and they're paying attention to you.

When I decided to write this book, I thought, yeah I've been through everything. Boy was I wrong! For the next several years, I wouldn't write any book. I would be put through my paces. It was as if God said, "Hey, you've still got some things to learn." And it was frustrating at times because it delayed my book, I was struggling and trying to figure it out. It allowed me to reflect on a lot over many months. It made me more aware of this bizarre love–hate relationship that I had with the movie business. And I realized, wow, I think a lot of people might feel this way! That's where I found a lot of my inspiration in writing this book.

Almost instantly after moving to Los Angeles, someone very wealthy was attracted to me. They told me that I didn't have to work if I didn't want to, and that they would take care of me. Of course it came with one big detail. I would then be in a relationship that would not be my choice with a man 30 years older than me. I was 19 years old and I was being exposed to wealth on a grand scale.

I knew my boundaries and I was ready for the journey into the movie business. I would wander onto movie sets and smoke cigarettes with the lead actors. This was of course before Homeland Security, and none of this would be possible now. But to me it was like watching an episode of the *A-Team*. I mean heck, when I took the Universal Studios tour, they told me that Steven Spielberg snuck into the lot and opened up an office.

One of the first big movies I got to work on, I wasn't even doing makeup. I was acting in a bit part with Robert Downey Jr. in a film called *Short Cuts*, directed by Robert Altman. It was a big experience but not a big paycheck.

How we relate to getting money has changed dramatically. Now it's like a conquest. We are literally conquering. We're already using terms like *kill it* and *crush it*. I destroyed them. But it gets even more interesting.

WE HAVE BEEN PROGRAMMED TO BELIEVE THAT OUR BANK ACCOUNT DETERMINES OUR WEALTH, EVEN AT THE RISK OF OUR HEALTH.

And the problem with that is that it doesn't just determine our wealth; we let it bleed into all kinds of other areas. We give it all kinds of power. We tie it to what we wear, what we drive. And we're often afraid of it. Oh, I'm still talking about wealth. Because even when you're wealthy, there's a fear, or a concern, of how long you can sustain it. Even with unlimited wealth, life can get boring fast if the ego isn't always at the wheel.

When wealth is present, the pressure is on. And let's talk about those people that like a little bit of pressure. A little bit of pressure? I think you mean a lot of pressure. The fact is many of us know that we operate really well under pressure, sometimes even extreme pressure. So we welcome it, but we welcome it so we can perform well? How does this really make sense?

Doesn't it make more sense to just be a professional, and be great at what you do? When you're focused and doing your thing, you should be in the zone regardless of any pressure. And you know what else is funny? When I hear people say, "I need a little pressure." What happens is they put themselves in a situation where they've got a little bit of pressure, but if it gets out of hand, then what? It's not like a Starbucks coffee that you order a certain way. How do you say I just want a little bit of pressure or I just want enough pressure? When real money is at stake and it's a job that's meaningful to you, there's already going to be natural pressure.

At one of the peaks of my career, I bought a house that was about $1.2 million, with a beautiful view. Even though I felt like I had made it, and I had the house and everything that came with it, there was incredible pressure. Just the $13,000 a year in property tax made me nervous. Maintenance and utility bills were in the thousands every month. Like we talked about earlier, when you get more, it comes with more, of everything.

Since you are in control, I would encourage you to skip the pressure. Instead, get creative, do it your own way, whatever that is. What does it look like with no pressure? What's it look like with total freedom allowing you to do whatever your skills and talents are? What if you just told your team from the beginning, "I just want to be able to direct, or act with no unnecessary pressure or distractions." What does that look like? If you can only perform well under pressure, what does the say about you? Are you creating your own pressure on purpose? I guess pressure can accelerate purpose, and if that seems to work for you, great. It's important to do what works for you. I found that when it's a healthy choice, the longevity of your career increases exponentially. Chances are your profits will too.

WHAT IF YOU COULD JUST PERFORM GREAT WITHOUT THE DRAMA AND PRESSURE? THESE ARE THE QUESTIONS THE VOICE OF CREATIVE HEALTH ASKS.

The filmmaking lifestyle is a funny one. We use military terms in our language when we're on set, like "copy that." I've even heard crew members refer to non-film people as "civilians."

There's no doubt that being a successful filmmaker requires a high-performance individual. That means you've got to be like an exotic car; you've got to be special and stand out from the bunch. And just like an exotic car, it's design is very different. Why? Because it's a high performer, just like you. If you put the wrong wheels on it, it destroys the performance. One small adjustment can not only cost time and money but also be a fatal mistake. More care goes into making an exotic car, and the price reflects it. What you bring to every project is unique. A lot of care has been put into you and where you're at. You are special, and like an exotic car, *your rate* will reflect that too. I really want to encourage you to feel good about your value. Think about all the enrichment and value you bring.

Even when you do really well and make lots of money, sometimes people still hate on you. Think about your favorite celebrity or musician. Now think about what it takes to be them as a lifestyle. Think about all of the trainers, the food, the coordinators and managers that help make that person who they are on the daily. This allows them to be a high performer, especially if you're in the face and voice of the business. When you look at the strategy and daily routines that celebrities have, you'll see how they're able to maintain consistency through practice and support. Just like we're doing right now.

We need to take note of this. And I'm not talking about the fluff and lies that are in the magazines and terrible TV shows. I'm talking about doing it on your level. Think of it as gearing up for production for yourself. Start with choosing your department heads. And you might be saying I don't have the money to hire a personal trainer or a team like celebrities do. That's OK. To begin, you can do it yourself. You're the director, the writer and the star of your own story. This is where you map out your dream. You can make adjustments along the way to the budget and schedule the same way you do with your projects. Because you are a project that's under constant development. And without you none of this is possible. Don't be so focused on perfection. Instead, love yourself, get what you need to be your best and bring *that* to the creative circles.

KEEPING FOCUSED

We talked earlier about focus and how important it is to not get so hung up on the multitasking myth. We talked about the kind of people you'll be dealing with that have difficulty focusing. And some of these people are in a leadership role. I want to be clear that I'm not getting down on anybody with a disorder. Many of my close friends and even family have these disorders. I've personally dealt with these disorders in my own life and had to incorporate solutions into my own personal practice. Remember, these are the people that will often admit, "Sorry, I'm super ADD, but I'm listening." Actually, only a small percentage of you is listening; the rest of you is elsewhere. When you consider that *time is money*, the qualities that come with someone in a leadership role really matter. If you come with a hard case of ADD and know it and do little about it, it adds serious risk. Just look at the description of ADD:

ADD, *attention deficit disorder*, is the term commonly used to describe symptoms of inattention, distractibility, and poor working memory. -Attitudemag.com

How about OCD? I hear that one a lot too. People claim it, like they won a prize. Here's its definition:

OCD, *obsessive-compulsive disorder*, is characterized by unreasonable thoughts and fears (obsessions) that lead to compulsive behaviors. -Attitudemag.com

I wanted to define these and talk about them because I'm not so sure that people really understand them. Even I don't fully understand them. But it's important to realize what we're saying when we throw these into our own description to others. These are disorders that run rampant in our business. They're frustrating to deal with and usually cost more time and money. After reading these descriptions, I hope that you'll think twice about claiming either of these. If you're leading with this often or repeating it to people frequently you're making it a reality. As we write our perfect life scenario, be careful about keeping these alive inside the story we're telling people and telling ourselves. And now that you're more aware of exactly what these disorders are, you can be more strategic when hiring people that make them known to you. It'll allow you to design better strategies, with fail-safe support.

If you're not doing anything to help these disorders, it's important to know some things. It won't just affect the business side with time and money, it'll affect the creative side as well. It affects everything, that's why it's a disorder—there's no order to it. The solutions are in what we've already talked about: staying focused, giving your full attention and listening. We can all be better at this. Remember, it's a practice. It's not about perfection; it's something you practice daily.

There were many people that I'd known over my lifetime that are no longer alive. And I can honestly tell you I'm glad that I've had this awareness and I gave them my full attention. When I look back, every time I was busy with some silly production demands or set drama, it would try to take away from those very important moments. By having this wisdom, you can now protect those people and those moments. And you should treasure them because they are treasures. Don't jeopardize precious family time and other moments with work drama. Don't be a slave to your phone. Creativity is all around you; when you're not distracted, it comes to you more freely. Your creative health is a priority, and by keeping it up, you'll have creative wealth too.

CHAPTER 9
HIRE YOURSELF

 Hire yourself, seriously. Look at the benefits.

You're the boss.

You get to do it the way you want.

You create great value.

When it's not working, you make it better.

Create something out of nothing? No problem.

And people love working with you.

When you believe in yourself, it makes sense to hire yourself. Why wouldn't you, right? Otherwise you'd be betting against yourself.

DOUBT IS A POWERFUL FEELING THAT CAN EASILY LEAD TO FEAR.

My dad was a big doubter, so I had early exposure. He was doubting for the right reasons, but the delivery was often poor. What I mean is his intention was to not take unnecessary risk and to keep his family safe. But if he did it in an angry way, it spoiled the good in what he was trying to do. It was hard to see that as a kid. The anger and the frustration are what I remember the most. As an adult, I still have to make it a practice to not do that in my life. I see it all around me. I see people struggle with it. Frustration and anger override them in the moment. They get me sometimes too. They get everybody once in a while. When you're aware of it, and you know you have a choice, that's when you're really in charge. It means someone else is not choosing for you; *you get to choose*. Even if your project gets held up or hijacked, there are still lots of choices, good choices too. You just have to know how to look and listen for them, remember? When you get creative with what you learned earlier in the book, you'll start to see positive results. As a creative artist, it's important to get creative with everything. Not just with what's on the page but also with what's going on in your life too.

A movie crew inherently wants to please the director. A happy director is a happy crew. I try my best to be kind to people. My artist mood can get the best of me under pressure though. Do you know what I mean? Has that happened to you? When I feel that intensity or pressure, I remind myself that I know about this. I know how to manage it. I'm in charge; it's my choice. Am I going to react and make a "right now" choice or am I going to take pause and think?

When you get real awareness of this, you get real control of it. It doesn't mean you're perfect at it all the time. It's how superheroes are made. They're called moms, dads, doctors, nurses, teachers. You know them, and you may even be one. And they're some of the best storytellers as well.

IT'S DIFFICULT TO WRITE A GOOD SCRIPT BASED ON LIFE EXPERIENCE IF YOU'RE NOT EXPERIENCING LIFE.

My dad always reminded me it was important to be *where the action is*. When it came to making money, he was right. Even though we have Zoom and technologies like FaceTime, nothing will ever replace what filmmakers crave the most, which is hands-on in-person experiences. We love being on set, right?

Do you know filmmakers that commute up to 90 minutes or more to work every day? I'm going to cut to the chase and tell you that can be unhealthy over time. I respect the commitment, and the dedication gets the highest marks. But let's break it down and look at it from this perspective.

A typical day on set is 12 hours. That's if you're on time and you don't go over. If your commute is up to an hour and a half one way, that adds three hours to your day. That leaves you with 10 hours to sleep and do whatever you can squeeze in before falling apart. Then, getting up and repeating it again and again. Aside from the dangers of driving home excessively tired, this doesn't leave much time for life. It doesn't leave much time for friends, family, pets, anything. If you've adopted the lone-wolf mentality that you don't need any of that, have any of that, want any of that, that's OK. Right now, you're good. Moving on.

Some people have had great success managing this way. They work a short amount of time on a project and make a grip of money. And then they'll be off for a month or more if there's nothing else they want to do. If you train for this, it can work really well. It also allows you to hire yourself and do your own projects your way in between.

When you hire yourself, you get to choose even when you're convinced that you have no choice. You can list out all the reasons that you have no choice. I've seen filmmakers dig the biggest ditches in the world and jump right in the middle of them. I'm speaking from experience, of course. Our creativity can run wild when it comes to doubt.

When you hire yourself, you really have to examine the story that you're telling yourself. It really highlights the reasons why you spend your time doing a certain project and investing in it. That story will change with the bad and good experiences. But now you have a better idea of what questions to ask and how to listen differently. When you hire yourself, you are investing in ideas, your ideas. Feel good about running the scenario all the way through with your ideas. And then take a look at them, and then take a look at them next week. Are they still as appealing? What's different about them now that some time has passed? I found that after the initial excitement wears off, a real reality sets in. That's the work part.

AS ARTISTS, WE HAVE TO BE CAREFUL ABOUT HAVING TOO MANY CREATIVE BABIES AT ONCE.

I hated my first job. It was dirty and smelly work. But I didn't have to cut my hair and the hours were flexible. And I wasn't in a band. Here's the thing though. What I learned on this job made me the most money later in my life. I learned how to use tools and load trucks. That was priceless because everything I create and use today involves those things frequently. I can't imagine not knowing how to use hand tools. Or how to safely load a bunch of camera gear and lighting into a vehicle.

The story that my dad would tell me was that I didn't get any creativity from him because he's not a creative person. He was convinced I got all my creativity from my mom. Luckily I was able to tell him multiple times that actually he taught me some of the best tools in the world when it came to being creative.

Creativity comes from everywhere; it's all around you. Even if you're somewhere you don't want to be right now, it's there too. You just have to know how to look and listen. I have come up with some of the best characters in my scripts by meeting them in real life first. Real-life experiences inspire us all the time. Even our failures and mistakes can be written about and laughed at.

My good friend Mark has worked on all the classic, big movies. He's a great guy. He had a client that wanted a car rig attached to a Lamborghini. In other words, they wanted to mount a camera outside of the car and have it pointed at the driver. So you have to be careful that you don't scratch the paint, and that it's safe and secure. These contraptions also stick out sometimes two or three feet off the side of the vehicle. So you really have to know what you're doing. Anyway, the Lamborghini had a vinyl car wrap. It's a sheet that lies over the body panels of the car, and you can change the colors or add graphics. They were using suction mounts (which are big suction cups) to mount the camera outside of the car. But because of the vinyl wrap, the suction cups couldn't adhere securely. The only place to attach the suction mount safely was the windshield. Luckily, it was a pretty lightweight camera. Mark instructed everybody that the car could not be driven over 25 miles an hour. But naturally, like a lot of music videos, things got carried away. So in the middle of rush-hour traffic, the Lamborghini sped through the streets with the camera rig attached to the windshield. When they returned, the windshield was cracked—not exactly a happy moment for the client who knew they pushed too hard. I forget the exact cost, but I know it was well over $10,000 to buy a new Lamborghini windshield and have it installed. This whole experience took about six weeks of back-and-forth. The bottom line was Mark never got paid for that day at the studio, even though he had warned them. The producer actually tried to blame Mark and get him to pay for it. You can probably guess the rest. Mark is an experienced guy. He owns a studio. He's worked with James Cameron and Michael Jackson and helped make countless blockbuster movies. Yet, this is the risk that you can incur when you're in charge. Owning your own business sounds great, and it is great. But you still have to go to work every day. And you still have to come home from work every day, especially *if home is work or work is home.*

You quickly learn when you hire yourself, and you see the results from the front row. You learn your real value, you feel better and you make more money. This is the essence of being an entrepreneur.

DON'T STRIVE FOR PERFECT, THAT'S BORING AND PREDICTABLE. STRIVE FOR WHAT FEELS GOOD, AND WHAT IS GOOD FOR YOU.

It'll translate to your inner artist. It'll keep you healthy for a longer run. You'll be using the force to its fullest potential. Make sure you help others and spread the good word on *how you're doing it*.

CHAPTER 10

LIVE HAPPILY EVER AFTER

I love being on set. I love it so much, I've spent over 30 years on set. I've noticed how people sacrifice and work really hard the first half of their life to be famous or successful. And then the second half of their life they spend working at getting away from it. That's when they want to *really start living*. You've probably seen some of the struggles in documentaries, or you might even be facing some of them yourself. It's important to look at your goals and how the rest of your life fits in. Keep check on this as it evolves and changes. It's a good thing. It's called growth.

I've been in a relationship for over 17 years. Together we've run multiple businesses and made millions of dollars. I've bought lots of houses and owned dozens of expensive cars. It's not something that I'm bragging about; it's something I want you to know because I speak from experience. If I hadn't done all that, I probably wouldn't know what I'm talking about. So I'm not bragging; I'm simply wanting you to know I've been there, more than once. When I told people early on I was thinking of writing a book, some of them discouraged me. I'd hear things like "There's no money in writing books; they'll just take our jobs if we tell them everything." If I would've listened to them, you wouldn't be reading this right now.

YOUR PARTNER CAN MAKE YOUR LIFE HEAVEN OR HELL.

I have known Frankie for almost 20 years now. She's my soul mate. The absolute love of my life. Technically, we're not married. And when people ask, this is confusing, and they often don't understand.

They'd say, "I don't understand how somebody could be together for so long and not be married?" It was like we went off script. We didn't write it that way; it just kind of happened that way. We're the kind of people that always made our own path. We're entrepreneurs, we do our way and we can't stand to be away from each other for too long. I guess time does fly when you're having fun.

I've also been asked a lot about how I met Frankie. I hired her, back when I had my photography and graphics business. She was my production manager and also a Photoshop artist. We were friends for two years before we were in a relationship. In fact, we became best friends. We saw each other every day because we worked together. Then we'd go out to dinner after work. And we talked about work, we talked our journey, we talked about everything.. We could count on each other. And at the time Frankie was going through a divorce. I was also in a relationship that was less than ideal. So that's how we met. But it gets even more interesting.

Frankie and I connected in so many different ways. We were also so different, in so many ways. We got to share about what it was like growing up being artists. We got to find out what we each thought was *really cool* when it came to art, music, movies and life. What really happened was, the more we learned about each other, the more we really fell in love. I was a skinny White dude and Frankie was a cute little, chubby Latina. Sounds like a Netflix show, doesn't it?

I wasn't interested in kids; I was way too focused on my career. Frankie had three kids. I couldn't stand rap music, and I had a lot of growing to do. So what happened? The universe just punched me in the face. I ended up working often with some of the biggest rap artists in the world and became friends with many of them. Today, our family has three grandchildren. I'm still getting used to being called "Papa," which I chose over grandpa. It shows me how none of that was part of my plan at the time. But *somehow* that's how it evolved. I can honestly tell you that on that journey, nothing was what I thought it was. Some of the goals were right *at the time* but I was still getting better at ebbing and flowing with everything and everyone. The assumptions I made were often incorrect. As an example, I really got to understand the artistry behind rap music. It meant a lot to me that these artists trusted me and invited me into their circles. I was with some really tough people and I felt safe. I was often the only white guy there, and I was telling everybody what to do. When it came to the music videos, I was looking out for them and they were looking out for me. I never felt like I was in danger. That's something that's always been true about me. I've been able to work with so many different cultures. I really enjoy learning about what's important to people and helping them bring their vision to life.

What a lot of people didn't know was my real middle name is Lamar. It was nice to be able to share that and not be teased anymore. That was the universe winking at me.

NEWS FLASH: NOBODY GETS OUT ALIVE

People believe in a lot of different things. I know people that believe in nothing. They think that this is it and when you die everything goes black, game over. I've always believed in God, a higher power, and that there's an afterlife when we're done here on earth. Everybody gets to choose their version that works for them when it comes to spiritual belief. If your tribe believes something different than you, that's OK.

Don't worry if you're not getting support from your tribe. Sometimes people in your tribe do not promote going outside of the tribe. They have their own ideas of what they think would be best for you. This especially includes your film tribe. Does any of this sound familiar? Tribes are constantly looking at other tribes and judging them on what they think they're doing right and wrong. I got to see the contrast in my own tribe. My dad believed he was not artistic, and he was frequently frustrated with managing his anger. He made a good living and provided for his family very well. My mom was an artist in many different ways and was very patient. She also provided for our family very well. My mom wanted me to learn a musical instrument. My dad didn't really see the value in it. He didn't believe we were those kind of people. He also had a skewed perspective of artists in general. He expressed to me that they were gypsies living out of a suitcase, having sex with a bunch of people. You know how when somebody tells you something and you just want to prove them wrong? You know you're not like everyone else and you're meant to do something special in life? I had so many of those times growing up with my dad. Growing up there was violent fights, arguments and constant judgment and disapproval. What I learned is I had to stop carrying this. I had to quit telling this version of the story because the story needed to change. I had changed. I was seeing a lot of things differently now, especially since I had applied the things I've shared with you in this book. When I think about it now, I'm really grateful that my dad showed me that contrasting perspective. It wasn't exactly positive, it wasn't healthy and he was just the guy to show me that. It wouldn't have had the same impact if it was from anyone else. If you're carrying some experiences similar to this, it's important to keep them in check. Don't let ego or fear tell you a story that's prodding you with a twisted edge. And if you've been carrying a story like that for years, it's time to let it go. When you surrender to it and you release it, it's gone. Say it to yourself, claim it. Take your power back.

I was certified in Corvette Racing when I was 30. I remember sitting in the classroom on the first day and the instructor showed a picture of a driver in a turn. He zoomed in on the photo. "You see where he's looking?" he asked. "He's not looking in front; he's looking through the turn." *Wow!* I thought. This has stuck with me forever. He's looking *through the turn* so he can see where he wants to go. "You know why this works?" the instructor asked. "Because the car's going to go wherever you're looking. If you're in a high-speed skid looking at a tree, that's where the car's going."

As you grow, you start to see things from a different perspective. Ask yourself, *what does tomorrow look like if there's $10 million in my bank account?*

For several years, we've rented an apartment that has a resort-style living theme. It's a newer building and we're on the top floor. I spend a lot of time outside on the balcony, looking at the view. I see the people come and go. The birds and creatures that fly through the air from the fifth floor are always putting on a show. When I go down to the first floor, it's such a different perspective, especially since I've spent so much time looking at everything from the fifth floor. Frankie would inspire me by saying things like "We live on the fifth floor. We go down to the first floor to visit or do business, but we always return to the highest level." When people talked about a higher perspective, that was my every day, literally. I had my edit bay setup just a few feet away, and I could step outside anytime. I was where the action is. Most meetings and shoots were happening right around me. It was convenient and it was by design. We set up our lives so we could go anywhere whenever we wanted to. We didn't have to worry about the kids, the pets, leaving the air conditioner on or anything. Oh wait a minute, we have plants and we have hummingbirds. We can pretty much leave whenever we want, as long as someone feeds the plants and the birds. Other than that, there was nothing holding us here. We were not a slave to our house, and we carefully managed our finances so that we had more freedom than most. Think about how you're setting up your lifestyle to be able to come and go and have the freedom you'd like.

Always consider your partner, your soul mate or the person you're living with. As a filmmaker, your life is on the go, you're traveling, you're adventuring, you're having as much fun as possible. You may leave at a moment's notice and then return to see everyone and everything you left behind. This will happen often when you're working a lot. It's important to consider your partner. How is this lifestyle for them? And how long are they OK with it for? I found that when you start to take your life back, you make your business fit in. Rather than making your life fit into your business.

GAME CHANGERS

These are some of the biggest game changers for a richer, healthier and happier lifestyle. How you do them will have a big effect on your journey. And if you're not doing them yet, it's time to start implementing them. Take a close look at:

1. Whom you partner with

2. How you share wealth

3. Investing

4. Diversifying into other businesses that are just as fun and exciting to you

5. How you market, network and promote

6. How you recharge

7. Building great credit

8. Using good loans

9. Limiting liabilities

10. Leveling up your friends and clients

When you do these things, life gets better. You can borrow money at a great rate and buy just about anything. Sharing your wealth and investing in businesses outside of the movie business feels good. Life feels better because you've upgraded your friends and clients.

EVERYONE LOVES FEATURE FILMS.

I wrote and directed a feature film back in 2012 that's been sitting on the shelf. Naturally, when I tell people this, they say, "Why!?" which is the reason I don't tell everybody. I've spent years having that conversation with so many people and usually gotten disappointing results. But I'm more than happy to tell you about the film. It's a cute little comedy about a guy named Dick Little. He has a terrible job with an awful boss, and a ridiculously pretentious friend. One day, he saves a homeless man from getting hit by a truck, and everything changes. The homeless man gives him a magic stone and tells him to wish for whatever he wants. The next day he wakes up in a mansion with a girl of his dreams and everything he always wanted.

I wanted to do a family-friendly movie that was fun, with a good story. But like most movies, this project was no different. It was a film that was going to need another ten thousand or so dollars to finish correctly. It's a project that didn't have any major stars, and it was likely to break even at best. I made several attempts through the years with different people to try to get it off the ground and get it finished. But no matter what I did, it just wasn't going to happen. I know this sounds crazy coming from a guy who has all these resources and helps people with similar situations. I felt like I was fighting it and the timing was never quite right, so I surrendered to it. I know I haven't lost any more money, and I know I haven't lost any more time. And I know it's still a good movie. So that's OK with me. Anybody that's ever made a movie knows that they can be time and money vampires.

Am I ever going to finish it? While I'm not happy that the actors don't get to see all the wonderful work that they did, I would rather wait and do it correctly. I'd like it to be the way it's intended to look and sound rather than it be a compromised version of my first film.

What I'll probably do is finish it when the time is right and I can package it with one or two other projects. To me, it makes more sense. It will be a better film and a better journey. Instead of a race to the bottom to make no money, I'm taking the same advice I'm giving you.

When you embrace filmmaking wholeheartedly, it pays you back in so many ways. Not everything you do is going to be a huge success or a hit. Trust the process.

WE'RE OFTEN ANXIOUS AS ARTISTS.
THAT'S THE "LITTLE BIT OF PRESSURE YOU WANTED."

If a skinny white dude, whose middle name is Lamar, can do this, you can too. I am blessed. I've been on a lot of adventures. And I'm so glad that you came along with me on this one.

Remember, you're not living anyone else's life. This is about you. Do it your unique way; that's what's going to make it successful. You are writing your life, you're directing it and you're the star.

Download all the bonus materials at: creativehq.com/bonus